D1553905

ROYAL HISTORICAL SOCIETY
STUDIES IN HISTORY
SERIES
No. 23

# JOHN RUSSELL, FIRST EARL OF BEDFORD
## One of The King's Men

# Recent volumes published in this series include

17    The Parliamentary Agents: A History                          *D. L. Rydz*

18    The Shadow of the Bomber: The Fear of Air                     *Uri Bialer*
      Attack and British Politics 1932-1939

19    La Rochelle and the French Monarchy:                         *David Parker*
      Conflict and Order in Seventeenth-
      Century France

20    The Purchase System in the British Army                     *A. P. C. Bruce*
      1660-1871

21    The Manning of the British Navy during                  *Stephen F. Gradish*
      The Seven Years' War

22    Law-Making and Law-Makers in British History            *Alan Harding (ed.)*

For a complete list of the series please see p 146

J. Russell L:d Privy Seale.                                      with one Eye.

# JOHN RUSSELL, FIRST EARL OF BEDFORD

One Of The King's Men

Diane Willen

LONDON
ROYAL HISTORICAL SOCIETY
1981

The Society records its gratitude to the following,
whose generosity made possible the initiation of
this series: The British Academy; The Pilgrim
Trust; The Twenty-Seven Foundation; The
United States Embassy's Bicentennial Funds;
The Wolfson Trust; several private donors.

Printed in England
by Swift Printers (Sales) Ltd
London E.C.1

To my parents,
Abraham and Sarah Willen

# CONTENTS

Holbein Portrait of John Russell (Copyright reserved) *frontispiece*

Preface      viii

Abbreviations      xi

1   Henrician Courtier      1

2   Patronage and Friendship      29

3   Councillor and Critic, 1540-1549      44

4   Russell and the West      62

5   The Final Years      82

6   The Bedford Wealth      101

In Retrospect      127

Note on Manuscript Sources      131

Index      132

# PREFACE

John Russell, first Earl of Bedford, was active in Tudor politics for nearly fifty years. Not as important as a Wolsey, Cromwell, or Seymour, Russell nevertheless has his own significance for those interested in the Tudor system of governance. As one of Henry VIII's 'new nobles'. he belongs to that group of courtiers and councillors generously compensated for loyalty and service to the dynasty. Operating within the system shrewdly and conscientiously, he held a number of offices during his lifetime – gentleman of the privy chamber, comptroller, Privy Councillor, lord high admiral, and, for over a dozen years, lord privy seal. Whatever the office, however, he was expected to be versatile; like his colleagues, he exchanged ceremonial, military, diplomatic, and administrative roles in turn. Nor were his responsibilities confined to those of national administration. First as lord president of the Council of the West, then as lord lieutenant of the western parts, he was also very much involved in government on the local level, where he made a real contribution. At court he enjoyed contacts or friendships with the major figures of the period, including a most interesting relationship with Henry VIII. These connections, the distribution of his patronage, his very mode of success – all reflect the realities of the Tudor state. In a similar fashion, Russell's activities as landowner and landlord speak to the social and economic issues of his day.

Although several of his colleagues at court have been the subject of recent political biographies, Russell himself has received only passing attention from modern scholars. Earlier historical studies dealing with his career vary in quality from unreliable works in the nineteenth century to the respected scholarship of Gladys Scott Thomson in the 1930s. As archivist to the Bedford estate, Thomson wrote several books on the family's history. Her remarks on the first earl are perceptive but, often placing Russell in a familial context, she did not emphasize questions of political significance. Subsequent historians may well have been deterred from a biographical study because of problems with source materials. No private family papers have survived, and neither the Devon nor Bedford County Record Offices, which divide the estate records between them, have account books for the first half of the sixteenth century.

Despite such difficulties, enough scattered sources exist to reconstruct a useful history of Russell's public career and to trace many of his property transactions. As an active courtier and councillor, his name naturally appears in the State Papers and other official records collected at the Public Record Office and the British Library. The Cottonian Manuscripts at the British Library, for example, are valuable for his diplomatic missions in the 1520s. Exchequer records, most notably the particulars from the court of augmentations, reflect the growth of his estate and many of his activities on the land market; also helpful are a series of leases for his Tavistock property housed at the Devon Record Office. Excerpts from the Exeter City Muniments together with random documents at the Devon Record Office and the Bedford Office in London provide information about his actions in the west. Research by the History of Parliament Trust has established details about the distribution of his patronage and his circle of friends. Imperfect though the sources may be, taken together they tell Russell's story and convey a sense of the man.

I have attempted to keep to a minimum the general historical narrative and yet see Russell within his political context. The chapters dealing with his last fifteen years of service are especially full, reflecting his increasing prominence at court. Chapters II, IV and VI depart from the chronology of his life to treat recurring themes, namely his friendships and patronage, his association with the west, his situation as landowner and landlord. Throughout I have depended upon the innovative and skilful scholarship of those historians who in recent years have greatly extended our knowledge of the Tudor period.

While pursuing this project, I have received advice and encouragement from many friends and scholars. I am indebted to Professor Nancy Roelker for directing the study in its preliminary stages and for sharing with me her enthusiasm for the sixteenth century. I am grateful to Professor Conrad Russell, who gave me invaluable assistance and guidance; to Professors Wallace T. MacCaffrey and W. K. Jordan, who, like Professor Russell, were kind enough to read my dissertation and offer suggestions; to Professor S. T. Bindoff, who welcomed me into his seminar at the Institute of Historical Research and made it possible for me to consult the unpublished files of the History of Parliament Trust; to Professor G. R. Elton, who read the manuscript and whose comments very much helped me prepare the final version. Mr. Alasdair Hawkyard has been a good friend, providing all kinds of useful information, several references, and kind, constructive criticism. I have benefited greatly from conversations with Professor Joyce Youings, Dr. David Starkey, and Dr. Katherine Wyndham, all of whom generously shared information and knowledge with me. Especially I owe thanks to Professor Joseph O. Baylen, whose encouragement and counsel have been indispensable, and to Dr. Daniel Traister, who has given many hours of his time to read the manuscript and suggest stylistic improvements. I am also pleased to thank a number of colleagues and friends for their assistance with the manuscript in its later stages. Dr. Michael Alexander, Dr. Steven Crow, and Dr. Carolina Lane helped me rework and strengthen individual chapters. My husband, Mr. James Roby, and also my sister, Miss Debra Willen, and my good friends, Dr. Barbara Traister and Dr. Virginia Hein, have mixed their editorial suggestions with much appreciated moral encouragement. Any errors in the work are, of course, my own responsibility.

Like all who do research, I have profited from the help and co-operation of numerous librarians and archivists. I wish in particular to thank the staffs at the Devon and Bedford County Record Offices, the Public Record Office, the British Library, the Bedford Office in London, the Institute of Historical Research, the Widener Library at Harvard University, the Woodruff Library at Emory University, and the Pullen Library at Georgia State University. I am grateful to the Trustees of the Bedford Settled estate for permission to consult and quote from the papers of the first earl; to the Marquis of Bath for permission to quote from the Seymour Papers; to the editors of the *Journal of British Studies* for permission to reprint in Chapter IV material which originally appeared as an article in the *Journal.* I wish also to acknowledge with appreciation the support provided by Georgia State University which facilitated the completion of the manuscript.

Atlanta, Georgia                                          D.W.
December 1979

# ABBREVIATIONS

| | |
|---|---|
| Add. MSS. | Additional Manuscripts, British Library |
| *APC* | *Acts of the Privy Council,* vols. I-V, *1542-55,* ed. John Dasent (London, 1890-92). |
| BL | British Library, London |
| BRO | Bedford County Record Office |
| *Cal. Pat. Rolls* | *Calendar of the Patent Rolls Preserved in the Public Record Office,* vols. I-VI, *Edward VI, 1547-53* and *Index;* vols. I-11, *Mary and Philip, 1553-55* (London, 1924-36). |
| *Cal. S.P. Dom.* | *Calendar of State Papers, Domestic Series, of the Reigns of Edward VI, Mary, Elizabeth,* vol. I, *1547-1580,* ed. Robert Lemon (London, 1856). |
| *Cal. S.P. Milan* | *Calendar of State Papers and Manuscripts Existing in the Archives and Collections of Milan,* vol. I, *1385-1618,* ed. Allen B. Hinds (London, 1912). |
| *Cal. S.P. Spain* | *Calendar of Letters, Dispatches, and State Papers Relating to the Negotiations between England and Spain,* vols. I-XIII, *1509-58,* ed. G. A. Bergenroth, *et al.* (London, 1862-1954). |
| *Cal. S.P. Ven.* | *Calendar of State Papers and Manuscripts, Relating to English Affairs Existing in the Archives of Venice,* vols. II-V, *1509-34,* ed. Rawdon Brown (London, 1871-73). |
| *DNB* | *Dictionary of National Biography,* ed. Sir Leslie Stephen and Sir Sidney Lee, 22 vols. (London, 1917). |
| DRO | Devon County Record Office |
| Harl. MS. | Harleian Manuscript, British Library |
| HMC | Historical Manuscript Commission |
| *L.P.* | *Letters and Papers, Foreign and Domestic, of the Reign of Henry VIII, 1509-47,* ed. J. S. Brewer, James Gairdner, and R. H. Brodie, 21 vols. and addenda (London, 1929-32). |
| PRO | Public Record Office, London (See Manuscript Sources for classes of documents). |

Numbers included in calendar citations refer, whenever possible, to documents rather than pages. All dates are given according to the New Style and indicate years beginning in January and ending in December.

# 1

## HENRICIAN COURTIER

John Russell left it to his descendants to show enthusiasm for their family's history. He was reluctant to speculate over the obscure past. Why should he have bothered? Like most good Henrician politicians, he instinctively preferred the concrete to the abstract, the real to the hypothetical. Befriended by the Tudor monarchs, assisted especially by Henry VIII, he eventually entered the ranks of the nobility, built the Bedford fortune, and established the Russells as one of England's foremost families. Under these circumstances, an impressive genealogy was an unnecessary luxury. But later generations, more accustomed to their status, expected – and accordingly found – more in their past. In 1626 the third Earl of Bedford produced an illustrious pedigree tracing the family origins to Hugo de Rosel, a companion of William the Conqueror. Diligent but misguided research in the nineteenth century strengthened this claim, and not until the early twentieth century did new studies expose its inaccuracies. The pedigree has since shrunk so that scholars now agree that they can trace the family with certainty only to the fourteenth century.[1]

The first direct descendant who has been clearly identified is not Hugo de Rosel in 1066 but Stephen Russell, probably born in the 1370s, four generations before John. The Russells at that point engaged in commercial and parliamentary activities and, by the eve of the sixteenth century, were members of the well-established gentry. They represent a classic textbook example of those solid, prosperous citizens who would eventually ally with the Tudor monarchs.

Quite a bit of information has been gathered about Stephen Russell and his son Henry, indeed much more than is known about John's father and grandfather. The earlier generations were prominent because of their participation in local and national politics. Stephen and Henry came from Dorset and had ties with the town of Dorchester as well as the seaport of Weymouth. In the fifteenth century they served as

---

1 See Gladys Scott Thomson, *Two Centuries of Family History; A Study in Social Development* (London, 1930), pp. 179, 30; Joseph Hulme Wiffen, *Historical Memoirs of the House of Russell from the Time of the Norman Conquest* (London, 1833). I; Joseph Horace Round, *Studies in Peerage and Family History* (London, 1901), pp. 250-78. Also Gladys Scott Thomson, *Family Background* (London, 1949), Chapter IV.

bailiffs and sat as Weymouth's parliamentary representatives. In addition to his responsibilities as burgess for Weymouth, Henry held commissions from the crown to collect taxes and patrol against smugglers. Nevertheless, politics remained a secondary concern, for these early Russells were primarily merchants. They sometimes adopted the surname of Gascoigne as an alias, probably reflecting their interest in the Bordeaux wine trade, and Henry Russell's property included a ship of sixty to eighty tons.[1]

Most English merchants received a serious setback in 1453 when the Hundred Years War ended with terms detrimental to English influence on the continent. But the Russells' fortunes, rather than declining, now took a new direction, growing more manorial and less mercantile. Even in the beginning of the fifteenth century, the family owned some land. Stephen Russell seems to have controlled certain houses in Weymouth and, more to the point, he made a profitable marriage. Through his wife Alice the family gained lands called Blintfield, closes in Stour Provost, a tenement in Dorchester, and a reversionary claim to the Dorset manor of Berwick. Henry Russell, following his father's example, acquired lands through marriage, and by the time of Henry's death in 1463 the family holdings had spread to Somerset.[2]

The first Russell to enjoy actual possession of all the property was Henry's son, John's grandfather, himself called John Russell. A knight for the shire in 1472, this elder John had at least three sons: Thomas, who apparently became involved in business ventures; Henry, a priest; and James, his heir, a gentry figure who inherited Berwick and begat John, the future earl. James married twice, had John by his first wife, Alice Wyse, and also fathered a daughter Thomasine. The Wyses of Sydenham were a respectable gentry family, and on his mother's side too John's relatives had sat in Parliament.[3]

The birth of John is usually assigned to the year 1485, but little is known of his childhood or education. He is not likely to have entered

---

1 Thomson, *Two Centuries of Family History*, p. 115; *Family Background*, pp. 218 ff. Dr. Linda Clark of the History of Parliament Trust has drawn my attention also to William Russell, a relative who sat for Dorchester in the Parliament of 1348.

2 Christopher Trent, *The Russells* (London, 1966), p. 36; Thomson, *Family Background*, pp. 230 ff. Alice Russell was heiress to the family of de la Tour who, Thomson suggests, owned Berwick as early as the reign of King John; *Family Background*, p. 242.

3 Thomson, *Family Background*, pp. 208-21; J.J. Alexander, 'Tavistock in the Fifteenth Century', *Report and Transactions of the Devonshire Association for the Advancement of Science, Literature, and Art* 69 (1937), 268.

either a university or the inns of court, paths that the gentry were not to follow in large numbers until the Elizabethan age. Thomas Fuller in the seventeenth century claimed that Russell was 'bred beyond the Seas' and, in fact, John could easily have travelled or studied abroad as an adolescent. His family still owned property in Weymouth, where he might have been acquainted with foreigners, and the Russells' commercial ties might also have encouraged him to embark for the continent.[1]　While there he would have enjoyed cosmopolitan experiences, explaining his fluency in French and Italian and the self-confidence and sophistication that enabled him to function successfully at the Tudor court.[2]

Russell's linguistic talent probably introduced him to the English court in 1506. In January of that year, Philip, Archduke of Austria and King of Castile, and his bride Joanna were forced to make an unexpected landing at Weymouth when a storm at sea interrupted their journey to Spain. Henry VII soon learned of their inadvertent arrival and eventually received the royal couple at court. In the meantime the pair had been welcomed and entertained by local Dorset gentry, including Sir Thomas Trenchard. Contemporary narratives record these events; tradition then adds that Trenchard called upon the young John Russell to act as interpreter for Philip and perhaps to accompany the royal pair to London. So well did Russell

Thomson includes a full genealogical chart in *Two Centuries of Family History*. p. 315. In abbreviated form the family tree reads as follows:

Stephen Russell of Weymouth,　　m　　Alice de la Tour of Berwick
　(d. 1438)

Henry Russell of Weymouth,　　m　　Elisabeth Herring
　(d. 1463)

John Russell, Esquire of Berwick,　m　　Elisabeth Frockmer
　(d. 1505)

James Russell, Esquire of Berwick,　m　　Alice Wyse of　　Henry　　Thomas
　(d. 1505/1506)　　　　　　　　　　　Sydenham
　　　　　　　　John　　　　　　　　　　Thomasine

John Russell, the first earl, was at least aware of this much of his ancestry. The heraldic arms he used included the coats of the Wyse, Frockmer, and de la Tour families as well as the lionhead of the Russells. See BRO, Box 262, [Thomson], 'Chenies, The House', pp. 8-9. Also Thomson, *Two Centuries of Family History*, p. 180.

1　Thomas Fuller, *The History of the Worthies of England* (London, 1662), (I), 281; I am grateful to the History of Parliament Trust and to Professor S.T. Bindoff for this reference. Thomson, *Family Background*, pp. 212-13, 248 and *Two Centuries of Family History*, pp. 116-17.

2　In addition to fluency in French and Italian, some historians add Spanish and/ or German. E.g., J.A. Froude, 'Cheneys and the House of Russell', *Fraser's Magazine* 15 (July-December, 1879), 365. No documentary evidence substantiates the point.

supposedly perform these tasks that he won the favour of Henry VII and was subsequently appointed to the king's chamber.[1]

In all likelihood this is one legend grounded in fact. Sir Thomas Trenchard might easily have relied upon Russell for assistance. The two families had been connected by marriage in the previous generation, and Russell remembered the Trenchards later when in 1549 he purchased the wardship and marriage of Thomas's heir Henry.[2] The incident of 1506 thus fits neatly into a pattern of friendly contacts between the two neighbouring families.

At any rate, 1506-7 proved a decisive year for John Russell. At about this time he won recognition from the king and by 1509 served as a gentleman usher.[3] He also assumed a new position within his family when in late 1505 or early 1506 his father died.[4] John was not to come into full possession of all his patrimony until the death of his stepmother in 1523, but, along with his stepmother and uncle, he had been named as one of the executors of his father's will; he already enjoyed the use of Berwick and could negotiate and transact business on the basis of his inheritance. In a modest way then both his political and landed careers had begun by the reign of Henry VIII.

Once at court, Russell joined that group of Tudor subjects able to turn loyalty and hard work to political and economic advantage. He skilfully exploited his position as courtier and, ultimately, his political shrewdness, his friendships at court, and his relationship with King Henry VIII were to pay great dividends. Yet his success was a long time in coming. He entered royal service years before Anthony Browne, William Paulet, Edward Seymour, John Dudley, William Paget — all names linked with his during the late Henrician period. His was a prudent, cautious nature, and his career naturally reflected these qualities. His rise was very real but not all that sudden.[5] During his first two decades of service, he discharged his duties as a minor figure

1  BL, Cotton MSS. Vesp., C. XII, fols. 181-87; Fuller, *History of the Worthies,* (I), 281; John Bridges, *The History and Antiquities of Northamptonshire* (Oxford, 1791), II, 406.

2  Inner Temple Library, Petyt MS. 536, vol. 46, fol. 438; PRO, Wards 9/154.

3  *L.P.;* I(i), 20, p. 12; cf. also HMC, *Various Collections* (London, 1903), II, 307 and below, p. 5.

4  James Russell's will was dated 30 November 1505 and proved on 15 February 1506; 4 Adeane (Prob 11/15/4). The date of his death is incorrectly given as July 1507 in Joan Russell's inquisition post mortem; PRO. C 142/40/28, 48. See Thomson, *Family Background,* p. 208.

5  Cf. Thomson, *Two Centuries of Family History,* p. 129.

on the periphery of political power and consequently left little or no trace in official records. He began as an inconspicuous courtier in the royal household, served next in military and administrative posts at Tournai, and returned to court only to embark, in the 1520s, first on a military expedition, then on a series of diplomatic missions. These years were neither particularly glamorous nor financially rewarding, but Russell used them to good effect. He worked diligently, came to the attention of Henry VIII, built a good relationship with Cardinal Wolsey, and earned the appreciation of both men. By 1526 he had to his credit a profitable marriage and a strategic appointment in Henry's privy chamber; by 1536 he had entered the king's Privy Council.

Russell's early years at court are especially shrouded in obscurity. The best evidence about his status comes from a directive which Henry VIII issued no later than 1513 to Sir Gilbert Talbot, governor of Calais. The king ordered the appointment of 'our trusty and wel-biloved servante John Russell, gentilman huissher of oure chambre' to a position in Calais.[1] Russell seems to have acted as usher at least since the funeral of Henry VII and, like many other figures at court, was retained by the new king. He may have served as one of the four ushers who, although excluded from the privy chamber, nevertheless performed well-defined tasks surrounding the king's person. But more probably he was called usher in a general sense as one of several lesser officials in the household who served 'out of wages' and whose names do not appear in the chamberlain's account.[2] In either capacity, he found the household an ideal place to meet the right people and establish valuable contacts. Himself a young man, only six years older than Henry VIII, Russell probably adapted easily to the new king's court and participated in the usual round of masques, pageants, tournaments, and dances. Henry's directive to Talbot, although using standard phraseology, commends Russell's service and makes it clear that the courtier had come to the king's attention.

Henry wanted Russell to serve as a spear in Calais. He expressed 'marveile' that his earlier command to that effect had yet to be acted upon and repeated his orders that Russell be granted a room within the

---

1  HMC, *Various Collections* (London, 1903), II, 307.

2  PRO, LC 2/1, fol. 120 or *L.P.*, I(i), 20. Russell of Dorset is cited as gentleman usher out of wages in PRO, S.P. 1/3, p. 78 or *L.P.*, IV(i), 1939(8). The document is classified with the Eltham Ordinances of 1526, but Dr. David Starkey has suggested to me that it is of an earlier date. Russell is not identified as a knight, substantiating Dr. Starkey's opinion. He is not to be confused with that John Russell granted an annuity in 1509 and identified as clerk of the court of Makesey; PRO, S.P. 1/1, fol. 45.

garrison, a salary of 8d. per day, and four men of his own. Talbot complied. When Henry arrived in Calais with the English army in June of 1513, Russell was among those on hand to greet the royal retinue.[1] During July and August, he may well have participated in the sieges of Therouanne and Tournai, English victories in Henry's first war against France. He subsequently spent much of the next five years on the continent, serving as one of the fifteen captains in the Tournai garrison during the city's English occupation.

Despite its initial and superficial success, the Tournai episode proved costly and counter-productive for the English. Russell shared in the accompanying dissatisfaction. He and the others stationed in the garrison found their task increasingly uncongenial as they saw their pay fall in arrears and felt themselves more and more isolated. Different groups in the garrison even wrote letters of protest in May 1518, a move apparently orchestrated by the English governor of the city. The king had just proposed biannual salaries at Tournai, a practice already established in other garrisons. The men at Tournai were dismayed and argued against the change, citing the problems unique to life in their garrison: provisions were dear in Tournai, English money continually declined in value, credit was difficult to come by, and friends were few. Russell's was the first signature on the letter of complaint which the gentlemen captains addressed to Wolsey.[2] And years later, in very different circumstances at Boulogne, Russell cited Henry's various counter-productive campaigns in France, a reference indicating his own displeasure with the Tournai venture.[3]

Nevertheless, though unhappy, Russell managed to advance his career during the occupation. As a captain, he received 4s. per day and was responsible for approximately eighty men.[4] He served under three consecutive governors: Sir Edward Poynings, Lord Mountjoy, and Sir Richard Jerningham. But his real achievement was his ability to make a favourable impression on Henry and Wolsey in the performance of

1 Cf. HMC, *Various Collections,* II, 307 and *L.P.,* I(ii) 2049.

2 *L.P.,* II(ii), 3323; C.G. Cruickshank, *The English Occupation of Tournai 1513-1519* (Oxford, 1971), pp. 100-102, 287-89.

3 PRO, S.P. 1/189, fols. 151, 153; see below, pp. 47-48.

4 Cruickshank, *The English Occupation of Tournai,* p. 99. Half-yearly rate cited in PRO, E 101/61/14. Cruickshank notes that each company usually consisted of a captain, petty-captain, and seventy-eight privates. It is not clear at what point Russell became captain. Although he is identified as a petty captain in a document of 1515 or 1516 (*L.P.,* II(ii), p. 1514), his salary is nevertheless cited as 4s. per day. The *DNB* does not recognize Russell's service in Tournai, an error based on a misdated document; *DNB,* XVII, 447 and *L.P.,* II(i), 2735.

even minor assignments. He came to Wolsey's attention in November 1515 when he participated in negotiations aimed against Richard de la Pole. Pole represented a danger to Henry VIII for, in addition to his role as Pretender, he was also in league with the king of France. Russell and a fellow captain, Thubianville, travelled to Lorraine to plot Pole's murder with the assassin Perceval de Matte. The project never materialized. Although de Matte had elaborate and impressive plans, his price was too high and the risk of failure too great for Henry to approve the undertaking. Yet Russell's activities had not been in vain: his work as a secret agent was duly reported to Wolsey.[1] A few months later, in May 1516, the king himself drew attention to Russell, directing that he construct a tilt yard, and in March 1517, Henry was pleased enough to grant Russell some lands in Tournai.[2] During the last year of the occupation, Russell continued to perform the miscellaneous tasks of a junior subordinate figure.[3] Early in 1519, he served as envoy to the Earl of Worcester, Henry's ambassador who made final arrangements for the English withdrawal from the garrison.[4]

Upon the restoration of Tournai, Russell's work abroad ended, at least temporarily. He was not re-assigned to his former post in Calais but instead, luckily, returned to court, always the most promising arena for advancing one's career. Russell re-entered the royal household. Almost immediately, significant changes occurred in the make-up of the king's privy chamber. In May 1519, Henry expelled several of his courtiers allegedly because they had led him into 'incessant gambling' and otherwise corrupted him. But the shrewd Venetian ambassador suggested a more plausible explanation for the removal of some of the king's companions. According to Sebastian Guistinian, the purge took place to make way for new men — Sir Richard Wingfield, Sir Richard Jerningham, Sir Richard Weston, Sir William Kingston — 'creatures of Cardinal Wolsey'.[5] Russell was not directly involved in these events. He

1 BL, Cotton MSS., Calig., D. VII, fols. 31-33 and Henry Ellis, ed., *Original Letters Illustrative of English History* (London, 1846), I, 202-12; *L.P.*, II(i), 1163, 1514.

2 PRO. C 82/434/8/18 or *L.P.*, II(i), 1907; *L.P.*, II(ii), 2982. Cruickshank remarks upon Henry's interference in the daily affairs of the Tournai garrison, *The English Occupation of Tournai*, pp. 51-55.

3 In February of 1518, Russell helped to intercept letters intended for the king of France, another cloak and dagger operation which produced no important results. See BL, Cotton MSS., Calig., E. 1, fols. 183-86; *L.P.*, II(ii), 3978; Cruickshank, *The English Occupation of Tournai*, p. 224.

4 Earlier Russell had travelled to England with messages for Wolsey. *L.P.*, II (ii), 4330, 4364, p. 1480; III(i), 58.

5 Rawdon Brown, trans., *Four Years at the Court of Henry VIII. Selection of*

now drew an annual salary of £33. 6s. 8d. for his position in the household, but he did not join the privy chamber[1] Nonetheless, he had come to Wolsey's attention during his years at Tournai and knew Jerningham well; the events of 1519 did his career no harm. By now, thirty-five years old, he had become part of the king's greater entourage, and in 1520 he was among those who accompanied Henry to France and the Field of the Cloth of Gold[2]

Like many of his colleagues at court, Russell turned from jousts and revels to war and soldiering in the spring of 1522. England had again allied with Spain to fight France. A naval expedition under the command of Thomas Howard, Earl of Surrey, set sail for Brittany in May. It included Russell, Jerningham, and several other members of the king's household. The English met resistance from the inhabitants of Morleaux but nevertheless pillaged the town and then proceeded to other havens along the Breton coast. After the battle of Morleaux, Surrey knighted Russell, Francis Bryan, Anthony Browne, Thomas More, and other members of the expedition for 'their hardyness and noble courage'[3] In Russell's case, the battle had been especially tragic and costly, for he lost the sight of his right eye in the engagement at Morleaux. The wound left a legacy though it was one not easily discerned by either contemporaries or subsequent historians. It may have contributed to that caution which Russell was to exhibit when given important military commands in later life, a caution which limited his effectiveness on the battlefield[4]

Yet his wound neither interrupted his career nor restricted his physical activities in any way. He remained a member of the expedition

---

Dispatches Written by the Venetian Ambassador, Sebastian Guistinian... (London, 1854), II, 270-71. Contrast BL, Cotton MSS., Calig., D. VII, fol. 118. Sir Henry and Sir Edward Guildford, Sir John Peachy, Sir Edward Neville, Nicholas Carew, Francis Bryan, and Francis Pointz were expelled. See David Starkey, 'The King's Privy Chamber, 1485-1547', unpublished dissertation, Cambridge University, 1974, pp. 80-112. Starkey sees a new office, gentleman of the privy chamber, emerging in the year 1518-1519.

1 L.P., III(i), 1114, p. 409. This salary, the equivalent of 50 marks, may reflect an annuity, perhaps given to Russell when his Tournai land grant was restored to the French. He continued to draw this salary throughout the entire decade; III(ii), p. 1543 and V, p. 305.

2 L.P., III(ii), p. 1555, Early in 1522, Russell received reversionary rights to certain customs and tolls, a sign of royal favour; L.P., III(ii), 2074(5).

3 Edward Hall, Chronicle, Containing the History of England . . . ed. Henry Ellis (London, 1809), pp. 641-43. John J. Nichols, ed. The Chronicle of Calais in the Reigns of Henry VII and Henry VIII, Camden Society, XXXV (London, 1846), pp. 31-32.

4 See below, pp. 26, 72.

until October when Surrey dispatched him with messages and requests to Wolsey.[1] Back at court, Henry and Wolsey made use of Russell's position as a gentleman of the chamber to convey intelligence to visiting foreign dignitaries.[2] His role at court became more clearly defined when, in June 1523, he was appointed knight marshal of the household, a figure responsible for excluding characters of ill repute from the confines of the court.[3] Like other household offices, however, the appointment was not primarily important for the actual responsibilities it entailed. In fact, after 1523 Russell was often away from court on official business and unable to discharge his official household duties. Rather the appointment signified the favour of king and cardinal and afforded opportunity for further promotion. Two months later, Russell was entrusted with a diplomatic mission, his most important assignment to date.

As the continental war against France expanded, Russell became involved, first, in the creation, then, in the maintenance, of a new alliance. Charles, Duke of Bourbon and Constable of France, was in conflict with King Francis I over French lands held by the duke's late wife. Henry VIII used the dispute to negotiate a treaty of alliance calling for an invasion of France in which Henry, the Emperor Charles V, and Bourbon were all to participate. The alliance with Bourbon took final shape in August 1523. Russell was a central figure in the negotiations, travelling incognito as a merchant through Luxembourg and Geneva before reaching Bourg. He returned to England with his mission completed by 20 September. As was customary, he was guided by a long and detailed set of instructions specifying the terms to which Bourbon should assent. Ultimately the treaty provided for English funds to finance Bourbon's war against France and also committed the English to invade before the end of August 1524. Wolsey wrote to his agents in Spain and explained that Sir John Russell had concluded the treaty as instructed. Only in one respect had Russell been unable to satisfy Henry's wishes: the duke refused to acknowledge Henry publicly as his liege lord and king of France. Henry was himself happy with Russell's performance. When Russell returned to court, More

---

1  L.P., III(ii), 2614.

2  Ibid., 2715.

3  Ibid., III(ii), 3139; Society of Antiquaries, A Collection of Ordinances and Regulations for the Government of the Royal Household (London, 1790), p. 154. The description of the office dates from 1526.

4  L.P., III(ii), 3217, 3307; State Papers during the Reign of Henry VIII (London, 1830-52), VI, 163, 174-75; BL, Harl. MS. 297, fols. 74, 115.

informed Wolsey that the king took 'great pleasure' from the envoy's 'well acheved errand'.[1]

Henceforth, from the failure of the triple invasion of France in the autumn of 1523 until Henry's break with the Imperialists in the summer of 1525, Russell's activities were closely integrated with the alliances and negotiations that consumed English diplomacy. His assignments reveal the harsh and dangerous demands made upon envoys in the sixteenth century. His responsibilities included transferring and often smuggling money; employing disguises and lies to guard against thieves and spies; and, of course, what has since become one of the traditional duties of a diplomat, receiving and giving intelligence reports.

By mid-October he was back on the continent with £12,000 to help pay ten thousand German mercenaries fighting on behalf of the Duke of Bourbon. Upon the advice of Margaret of Savoy, he enlisted the help of merchants, disguised himself as one of them, and, by early November, safely brought the money to the Imperial city of Besancon. But he was too late. The mercenaries had already dispersed. Shortly thereafter, Bourbon decided to travel to Genoa and join the emperor. Under these conditions, on 29 November, Wolsey wrote that the money should return to England via Antwerp.[2] Russell, however, did not learn of Wolsey's decision until early January. In the interval, during November and December, he worried about the safety of the English funds and the dangers posed by French spies. For safety's sake, he spread rumours that the money had already returned to England.[3]

Russell returned to England in late April, but his stay was short. Within a few weeks, he received another assignment to distribute English funds on the continent, this time £20,000 to the Duke of Bourbon, in southern France. Richard Pace was then the English envoy travelling with Bourbon's army. On 28 May Wolsey informed him of Russell's charge.[4] Pace felt that the money was vital to Bourbon's success and waited anxiously for its arrival. But in mid-June he learned that Russell was still at Antwerp, meeting unexpected delays. By July Pace complained of negligence, worried about mutinies, and curtly observed that 'one penny in time' was worth 'three out of time'. Yet not until late August did English funds reach Bourbon's army at

---

1  *State Papers*, I, 135; *L.P.*, III(ii), 3346.

2  *L.P.*, III(ii), 3399, 3440, 3498, 3525, 3571, 3578.

3  *Ibid.*, 3661; IV(i), 17. For copies of Russell's diplomatic dispatches, see the Bedford Office, London, Papers of the First Earl, 5.

4  *L.P.*, IV(i), 268, 374; *State Papers*, VI, 288-295.

Marseilles.[1] Russell's experiences during those summer months of 1524 may be taken as typical of the problems encountered in conveying and protecting funds. In Geneva, fearing robbery, he had hidden the money in bales of oats. Reaching Chambery in late July, he had taken still more precautions. In the guise of a merchant, he travelled ahead with mules now carrying genuine oats. Meanwhile the money was actually packed in coffers belonging to the Duke of Savoy and transferred as if the duke were moving furniture; quite an elaborate hoax but one that worked.[2] Russell's caution had worried Pace and slowed the money's arrival — yet his caution was probably necessary for it to arrive at all.

Because of haphazard communications during such operations an envoy often had to act independently and trust his own judgement. At times Wolsey simply did not have enough information at hand and explicitly appealed to the personal discretion of his agents abroad. Thus, he wrote to Russell and Pace in August, explaining that the king was sending an additional £10,000 with Mr. Weston, the Turcopolier of the Order of St. John. Once they received the money, Russell and Pace were to act on their own. 'Not knowing how thaffayres of the Duke of Bourbon shall succede', the king wanted the money available if its distribution would insure Bourbon's victory. But Wolsey added a note of caution: 'the king and I trust veryly you will not se yt uttered and spent in vayne, but to be reservyed . . . as the time and commodities shall, by your good discretion lead you'. Although anxious that the emperor pay his fair share before Russell and Pace committed more English funds, Wolsey was 'loathe to give over precyse instructions'. Changes in the situation were impossible to predict. Russell and Pace knew enough of the king's 'mind and intente' to know also 'how to governe the mattier to the kinges honnor sewrtie and profyt'.[3]

Russell on his part was not overeager to act independently of specific instructions lest his actions cause the king displeasure. After receiving Weston's money in October, he went on to Rome, apparently to ask the crown's agent there, John Clerk, what to do with the funds. In Rome he learned that Bourbon's army was retreating from Provence.[4]

1   L.P., IV(i), 422, 456, 471, 483, 503, 606; BL, Cotton MSS., Vit., B. VI, fols. 129-30.

2   BL, Cotton MSS., Vit. B. VI, fols. 150-51. To follow Russell's itinerary, consult L.P., IV(i), 433, 463, 542, 570, 608 and III(ii), 3168 and 3212, which are mistakenly dated as 1523. See also Jervis Wegg, Richard Pace (1932; rpt. London, 1971), pp. 232, 237, 245-46.

3   State Papers, VI, 332; L.P., IV(i), 590.

4   L.P., IV(i), 725.

One of the emperor's men, supported by the pope, then appealed to Russell for a loan and warned that the fate of all Italy hinged on the decision. On 24 October Russell reported to Wolsey and noted that the sum at his disposal was not so great. Still he refused to act without the king's 'express command'. It was not responsibility so much as unnecessary risk that Russell, always a cautious and prudent envoy, sought to avoid in such situations. He was resourceful enough to suggest options to Wolsey, including a way for the money to escape Imperial hands without provoking the emperor. Let the money return to England, Russell wrote, and 'your grace may lay all the fault on me saying that I did it without your prior commandment'.[1]

Russell remained on the continent through the summer of 1525. November and December he spent in Rome where he arranged for the exchange of the money. In January, when Wolsey sent instructions that the funds be given to the viceroy in Naples, the money was still in the hands of various bankers and merchants and not available for distribution. Wolsey further instructed Russell to join Bourbon's army in Pavia. Russell arrived there in early March, time enough to report on the final stages of the Imperial victory and the capture of Francis I.[2] Thereafter, until the end of July, he provided regular intelligence about Bourbon's movements, the allies' prospects, and negotiations with Francis. In the process he became an enthusiast for the duke and even provided him with military advice. Nonetheless, when Bourbon anticipated a journey to Spain in June, Russell saw no good reason to accompany him.[3] By now Russell was no doubt weary of his diplomatic chores and anxious to return home. Fortunately, the Spanish journey never materialized for him. A truce was concluded between the English and the French to begin 11 September, and by November Russell was back at court where he enjoyed a respite from his travels.[4]

Although Russell worked with a number of competent English envoys on the continent, Richard Pace was his most important colleague. Many of Wolsey's instructions in the summer of 1524 were addressed jointly to Pace and Russell, and both men were closely associated with Bourbon. Three years older than Russell, Pace had been in Wolsey's service since 1515, had frequently acted as one of Henry's secretaries and, by 1524, had engaged in diplomatic missions for nearly

1   BL, Cotton MSS., Vit. B. VI, fol. 219; *L.P.*, IV(i), 765.

2   *L.P.*, IV(i), 909, 923, 939, 942, 1017, 1045, 1085-86, 1175.

3   BL, Cotton MSS., Vit., B. VII, fols. 77-78; *L.P.*, IV(i), 1175, 1283, 1326, 1339-40, 1357, 1410, 1425, 1498.

4   *L.P.*, IV(i), 1556, 1744.

a decade. Pace was moreover a man of impressive intellectual standing, a humanist whose circle of friends included More and Erasmus. With such credentials, his opinions might well have carried more weight than Russell's. Nonetheless, Pace in 1524 was entering the final phase of his career and from this time on, both his influence and his health rapidly declined. For some reason Wolsey had already lost confidence in his loyalty and abilities.[1] The Bourbon assignment and Pace's subsequent enthusiasm for the duke aggravated the cardinal's displeasure. As Pace lost his objectivity, his value and influence at the English court diminished.[2]

Russell's position was in some respects analogous. He too came to admire Bourbon, attributing the victory at Pavia to the duke and forwarding to the English court Bourbon's request for additional funds.[3] King and cardinal followed Russell's advice no more readily than that of Pace. Though they were quite willing to exploit to English advantage the good relationship that existed between Russell and Bourbon, Russell remained a subordinate figure and his opinions were treated as such. Like Pace he was more likely to be informed of policy changes than to shape decisions.

Yet, in contrast to Pace, Russell's reputation at the English court grew increasingly secure. Wolsey's correspondence reveals no simplistic or obvious judgement of his subordinate. At times, displeased with Russell's actions, he reprimanded him, usually with a great deal of tact.[4] But the discretionary powers granted to Russell, the length and frequency of his assignments, and, in January 1526, Russell's inclusion in the Eltham Ordinance as a gentleman of the privy chamber — all indicate that Wolsey was happy with Russell's performance and confident of his loyalty. The friendship which the two men were to exhibit during Wolsey's fall from power in 1529 took root in these years. Henry VIII, for his part, also kept track of Russell's activities, for Russell took pains throughout this period to report faithfully to the king as well as Wolsey, sometimes writing identical letters to both men. His reward came with admission to the privy chamber, a sure sign

---

1   The causes of their estrangement were not certain, but Pace's assignments immediately preceding the Bourbon alliance had done him no good. He had been unsuccessful in 1521, promoting Wolsey's claim to the papacy, and again in 1523-24, trying to detach the Venetians from their French alliance. *DNB*, XV, 22-24; Wegg, *Pace*, pp. 263-64, 270-72.

2   See BL, Harl, MS. 282, fol. 287;   J.J. Scarisbrick, *Henry VIII* (Berkeley, 1968), 132-33.

3   BL, Cotton MSS., Vit., B. VII, fols. 77-78; *L.P.*, IV(i), 1175, 1339.

4   BL, Add. MSS. 5860, fol. 65 or p. 126.

that he enjoyed Henry's goodwill as well as Wolsey's confidence. At the age of forty-one, he had a promising career ahead of him.

Sometime between November 1525 and October 1526, Sir John Russell married. No personal family papers survive, and the marriage therefore retains, even more than usual, its share of secrets. But available evidence clearly suggests that, whether by design or accident, Russell's choice of marriage partner was among his shrewdest and most successful decisions, giving him an intelligent, compatible companion, a wife conscientious in familial responsibilities, a colleague well versed in the politics of the court, and an heiress with considerable property.

Anne Russell's financial assets, the most easily documented of her attractions, immediately improved her husband's status. The daughter and heiress of Sir Guy Sapcote of Huntingdonshire, she owned three manors — Chenies in Buckinghamshire, Thornaugh in Northamptonshire, and Covington in Huntingdonshire — worth together approximately £70 *per annum*. Russell appreciated Chenies in particular, for he adopted it as his country residence and almost immediately set about rebuilding and enlarging it. In addition to her own wealth, moreover, Anne was a widow. According to a valor in 1539, her jointure from previous marriages was worth £183. Russell must have welcomed the financial security which his wife brought him. He had sold portions of his patrimony, so that by this period his single most important piece of property was Berwick manor, valued at £33 in 1539. His sales suggest that he may have needed ready cash during his years at Tournai. Even in the 1520s, when travelling abroad, he incurred expenses which the crown did not always cover.[2]

The events of 1526 certainly improved Russell's financial standing. In addition to his most substantial gains, his wife's property, he also came into possession of Amersham manor, a wedding gift from Henry VIII; Amersham was not far from Chenies in Buckinghamshire and was itself worth more than £43 *per annum*. Moreover, Russell's new position as gentleman of the privy chamber included not only lodgings for himself but also herbage for his horses, bouche at court for two of

1   *L.P.*, IV(i), 1939, p. 863. Sir John Russell was also named in a grant of 1525 to be keeper and porter of Newport Castle in Wales, but this patent may well refer to Sir John Russell of Worcester; 1136(15). For earlier grant, see III(ii), 3507.

2   Valors are derived from PRO, E 315/418. See below, Chapter VI for a discussion of Russell's property. The crown did reimburse Russell for his 'diets' when abroad on official business; *L.P.*, IV(i), 1744.

3   *L.P.*, IV(ii), 2761(15).

his servants, and 'bourd wages' in town for a third servant.[1] By 1527, Russell's income, including both lands and fees, was assessed at £134.6s.8d., a conservative figure that seems to have reflected some of his wife's property but not her jointure. Incomes of colleagues who served with Russell in the household ranged from £66 to £400 *per annum.*[2] Even after his marriage, then, Russell's wealth was respectable but not at all exceptional.

Anne was already twice widowed before she married John. Her jointure was derived in part from the property of her first husband, John Broughton, whose will was proved in June 1519. Broughton left Anne with four children to whom he bequeathed a cash legacy of £700.[3] Three of the children survived at the time of the Russell marriage. In the interval, Anne had taken as her second husband, Sir Richard Jerningham, a figure whom Russell knew well. Contemporaries regarded Jerningham as one of Wolsey's men,[4] and both the cardinal and the king probably encouraged Russell's match with his widow. Her earlier marriages and Russell's forty-one years gave each a maturity that helped their relationship.

Like her husband, Anne Russell served at court. After 1528 the king often included her among the recipients of his new year's gifts, and during the 1530s and 1540s she attended Princess Mary. Her position at court made her sensitive to political realities and on occasion enabled her to combine shrewdness and influence to protect her husband's career. She judiciously distributed gifts – deer, swans, greyhounds – to her monarch and her long-standing relationship with Mary helped the Russells at the time of Mary's accession.[5]

Still, Lady Russell was far from totally absorbed in court pursuits and politics and, in fact, during the first years of her marriage to Russell, she was preoccupied with her children.[6] Probably in 1527 she gave

1 PRO, LS 13/278, pp. 125, 143, 152. Russell also continued to receive his annual salary of £33.6s.8d.; *L.P.,* V, p. 305.

2 *L.P.,* IV(ii), 2972.

3 17 Ayloffe (Prob 11/19/17).

4 Jerningham had served as Wolsey's diplomatic envoy and as vice-chamberlain of the household; *L.P.,* II(ii), 2819; III(ii), 3601.

5 *Ibid.,* IV(ii), 3748; XIII(ii), 1280 (f.55); XVI, 380 (f.110), 1489 (f.166b); Nicholas H. Nicolas, *The Privy Purse Expenses of King Henry the Eighth* (London, 1827), pp. 107, 245. In 1541, at the time of the fall of Katherine Howard, Henry ordered Lady Russell to house and guard Lady Rochford; *L.P.,* XVI, 1401.

6 Thomson sees Anne Russell as 'housewifely inclined'; *Two Centuries of Family History,* pp. 149-50.

birth to the only child of her third marriage, a son Francis, who was eventually to ensure the continuity of the Russell line. All was not idyllic, however, during these early years, for in 1528 John Broughton, Lady Russell's son by her first marriage, died. Her intense grief at his loss was aggravated by the prospect of losing custody of her younger daughter, whose wardship Russell thought in Wolsey's hands. Sir Thomas Heneage, formerly Wolsey's servant and now a colleague at court, helped the Russells plead their case. 'So sore' did the mother take the death of her son, Heneage explained to Wolsey, that Russell feared subsequent loss of the custody and marriage of her younger daughter would prove her 'uttre ondoyng'.[1] According to Russell himself, his wife looked upon her daughter as 'all her Joy in this world'.[2] In the end, despite such pleadings, the dispute was not resolved in their favour.[3]

Glimpses into the private lives of the Russells are too rare to support definitive conclusions but consistently suggest a harmonious family life.[4] Lady Russell's distress in 1528 was unique, the only time she publicly revealed any sign of weakness. Family memoirs picture her otherwise as a strong, forceful woman, a characterization supported by events of the 1530s.[5] His marriage, then, had improved Russell's financial situation and provided him with a stable, and apparently successful, personal relationship. He could pursue his political career with a new sense of personal security.

Russell's prospects at court were greatly enhanced when, along with Sir William Tyler, Sir Thomas Cheyney, Sir Anthony Browne, Henry Norris, and Nicholas Carew, he was named in the Eltham Ordinances of 1526 as gentleman of the privy chamber. Wolsey drew up the Ordinances to reduce personnel at court and ensure control over the

---

1  *State Papers*, I, 303; *L.P.*, IV(ii), 4436.

2  PRO. S.P. 1/49, fol. 63; *L.P.*, IV(ii), 4456.

3  The wardship-marriage dispute dragged on for a number of months. Appeals to Wolsey did no good, for the wards were discovered to be the king's, and other gentlemen at court, Sir Thomas Cheyney and Sir John Wallop, with their own influential friends, expressed interest. Although Anne Boleyn supported Cheyney's claims, Henry seems not to have taken sides, and the final resolution of the question may have represented a compromise. On 20 November 1529 the wardship was purchased by Agnes, Duchess of Norfold. Much later, in 1532, Cheyney and Russell argued over the details of the marriage settlement. *L.P.*, IV(ii), 4437, 4456, 4584; IV(iii), 5624(10), 6072(21), 6187(12); VI, 462.

4  See e.g., *L.P.*, XIII(i), 1491; XIII(ii), 431.

5  At one point in 1532, Russell sent her on an unusual but successful mission to collect funds owed him by the king which his own letters has been unable to procure; see below, p. 23.

politically sensitive privy chamber. He had learned to trust Russell during the latter's recent diplomatic assignment and Henry too had no trouble accepting his 'trusty and welbiloved' servant. Now as one of the six gentlemen of the privy chamber, Russell was charged with performing the monarch's most private service. Only these six gentlemen were allowed to touch the king's person and dress him; at least two of them were to spend the night in his privy chamber. And they, together with the Marquis of Exeter, Henry's kinsman, and two gentlemen ushers, four grooms, a barber, and a page, constituted the staff of the royal privy chamber, those meant to attend the king permanently.[1]

Russell remained a gentleman of the privy chamber from 1526 until 1539, when he was ennobled.[2] It was a position which maximized the usual advantages associated with a position of the household. It gave him increased opportunity to know Henry and cultivate his confidence; later he would use his accessibility to the king to advocate favours for friends and clients. In no way were his responsibilities limited to the ceremonial and menial tasks outlined in the Eltham Ordinances. As in other areas of the household, members of the privy chamber cared for the king's private affairs on the one hand, and on the other, engaged in public or state business. The nature of the privy chamber then reflected continuing confusion over the king's role as medieval lord and head of government. Yet in this very confusion Russell found opportunity. He often served as go-between for Henry and his ministers, acting by 1528 in a secretarial role.[3] With other gentlemen of the privy chamber, he was expected to know foreign languages in order to help receive foreign visitors at court and to conduct royal business abroad. Like his colleague, Sir Anthony Browne, with whom he sometimes lodged at court, and like many Tudor figures — Edward and Thomas Seymour, William Herbert, Thomas Cheyney, Ralph Sadler, Thomas Denny — Russell successfully used his position as courtier to acquire additional offices and increased responsibilities.

In January 1527, Russell was once again sent abroad on a diplomatic mission.[4] He probably did not fully understand the changes which

---

1  *L.P.* IV(i), 1939, p. 863; Starkey, 'The King's Privy Chamber', pp. 160-64, 312.

2  Russell was included in an order of 1532, which named fourteen gentlemen of the chamber and divided them into two groups that alternated service, each attending the monarch for six weeks at a time; *L.P.,* V, 927. The order was, however, not regularly enforced. See Starkey, 'The King's Privy Chamber', pp. 189-200. After 1536 Russell had other offices which demanded his attention.

3  See e.g., *State Papers,* I, 301-302; *L.P.,* IV(ii), 4422.

4  *L.P.,* IV(ii), 2769-70.

English policy had experienced since the intoxicating days of Pavia. After that Imperial victory, Henry's enthusiasm for a joint venture against France knew no limits, but Charles was reluctant to indulge Henry's fantasies. Moreover, the emperor rejected marriage with Princess Mary, Henry's last hope for an orderly succession so long as he remained married to Catherine of Aragon. Therefore, after concluding a truce with the French in August 1525, Henry and Wolsey encouraged the formation of the League of Cognac in the spring of 1526. The League, a continental alliance aimed against Charles and the Duke of Bourbon, included France, the papacy, Florence, Milan, and Venice. Its success would assure the papacy's independence from Imperial domination, a crucial goal for Henry as he contemplated divorcing Charles's aunt. Russell's assignment in January 1527 was to provide moral and financial support for Pope Clement VII and prevent a unilateral truce between the papacy and the Imperialists. As an alternative to a unilateral truce, he was to promote Wolsey's plan for a general peace under English auspices. It was not an easy task, especially given England's reluctance to commit itself militarily, and ultimately neither Russell's efforts nor English funds were to any avail.

Russell began his journey to the continent on 2 January, voluntarily accompanied by Sir Thomas Wyatt, whose long-standing friendship with Russell dated from this period.[1] They reached Rome on 6 February and were auspiciously received. The pope was most happy to see Russell who, after all, came with 30,000 ducats. An unknown writer, describing Clement's sense of relief, claimed that all of Rome sang with praise for both Henry and Wolsey.[2] Russell's own account to Henry confirms this picture. The pope asserted that he was more beholden to Henry than to any other prince and, according to Russell, everyone in Rome agreed that the English king had shown himself to be the true Defender of the Faith. Concluded Russell, 'I thinke verely Your Highnes never spent monney that shall sounde more to your honour than this'.[3]

On his arrival, Russell had been greeted by papal representatives who wanted him to reside within the papal palace. Russell wisely declined, realizing the jealousies which such special treatment might provoke among other ambassadors, and lodged instead with Sir Gregory Casale,

1  D.M. Loades, ed., *The Papers of George Wyatt Esquire*, Camden Society, Fourth Series, V (London, 1968), 27-28. The pair stopped in Paris so that Russell could visit Wolsey's illegitimate son, Thomas Winter, and inform Wolsey of Winter's situation. *L.P.*, IV(ii), 2805-6.

2  *L.P.*, IV(ii), 2870; cf. 2852-53, 2868.

3  *State Papers*, VI, 563; *L.P.*, IV(ii), 2876.

the English envoy in Rome. But Russell managed to remain on good terms with Clement and found the pope ready to follow English bidding if it were feasible for him to do so. Immediately he and Casale wrote that Clement was willing to follow Wolsey's advice and entrust peace negotiations to the cardinal; moreover, should mediation fail, Clement promised that he would prosecute a vigorous war.[1]

Although Russell again distributed English funds, as he had in 1524, this time he was involved primarily in diplomatic negotiations. He consulted with the ambassadors of the various principals in the war and promoted proposals drawn up by Wolsey and Henry. Within ten days of his arrival in Rome, following his instructions from the English court, he travelled to the town of Ciprane to negotiate with the Imperial viceroy of Naples for a truce favourable to the pope. Although Clement was ready to accept the Viceroy's offer by 23 February, Russell and Casale felt that the terms did not satisfy England's conditions. Hoping that Venetian aid would enable the papacy to prolong hostilities against Charles, Russell did his best to persuade Clement to confer with the Venetians before signing any truce. With the pope's approval, he set out for Venice on 25 February, only to break his leg on the trip. Wyatt went in his stead and extracted a pledge from the Venetians to contribute men and money to the war effort.[2] Clement, however, still insisted on unilateral action and accepted the viceroy's offer to suspend fighting, making Henry and Wolsey furious. When the papal nuncio claimed that Clement had acted with Russell's approval, Wolsey angrily replied that Russell had been given no such authority. In fact no documentary evidence survives to support the nuncio's claim. On 20 March, Russell and Casale assured Wolsey that they were following the cardinal's instructions: Clement had been informed of English unhappiness over the precipitous truce.[3] Yet Wolsey need not have worried. Because neither Bourbon nor Charles accepted the terms of the truce, Clement resumed hostilities by April. Russell and Casale, temporarily relieved by the turn of events, remarked that it was no small matter 'considering the popes ferefull nature to have returned hym to the war'.[4]

Throughout these months Russell demonstrated a greater sense of confidence and a greater willingness to assume responsibility than he

---

1   PRO, S.P. 1/48, fols. 1 ff.; *L.P.*, IV(ii), 2875.

2   *L.P.*, IV(ii), 2870, 2875, 2879, 2891, 2907, 2910, 2912, 2918-19, 2931.

3   *Cal. S.P. Ven.*, IV, 74; BL, Cotton MSS., Vit., B. IX, fols. 75-76 (85-86) or *L.P.*, IV(ii), 2971.

4   BL, Cotton MSS., Vit., B. IX, fol. 97 (106); *L.P.*, IV(ii), 3065.

had evidenced in his previous missions abroad. He willingly took the initiative as, for example, when he advocated a match between Henry's illegitimate son, the Duke of Richmond, and the pope's niece.[1] Although he was sympathetic to Clement's problems and the pope in turn trusted him to do diplomatic work on his behalf, nevertheless, Russell was realistic in assessing Clement. He never lost his detachment nor waxed as enthusiastic as he had done in 1525 over Bourbon. To alleviate financial pressures, Russell urged the pope to create new cardinals. The idea came from Wolsey who favoured the promotion of certain candidates. Clement hesitated. Not until May did he finally agree, seeing 'a perpetuall shame' in such simony.[2] Yet, on this issue, as on others, the pope's reluctance had been met and overcome by Russell's persistence. Russell showed similar firmness in dealing with Francis I. The Milanese ambassador claimed that the English envoy actually reproached the king of France, 'adjuring him in God's name to leave his hunting and ceaseless pleasures and attend the war, so that the enterprise may not be endangered'.[3]

As the continental war progressed — and, from the English point of view, deteriorated — events with momentous consequences for Anglo-Papal relations were occurring. In May 1527, a tribunal convened under Wolsey's auspices to question the validity of Henry's marriage with Catherine of Aragon. Nothing in his correspondence indicates that Russell was consulted in this matter or involved in its opening stages. He was at this time returning to England after requesting his recall as early as 29 March. Any number of factors may have made him anxious to return home: his recent marriage, the accident to his leg, a lack of personal funds, the deteriorating situation in Italy. When he finally departed in the last days of April, he carried with him a commission from Clement to plead 'the pope's necessity' to the French king. He left Rome just before the city was sacked and, on 11 May, wrote to Henry from Savona, expressing indignation and shock at the barbaric behaviour of Imperial troops. He seems to have been back at the English court by June.[4] In early January 1528, Henry and Wolsey

---

1 PRO, S.P. 1/48, fols. 3, 5-6; *L.P.*, IV(ii), 2875-76.

2 BL, Cotton MSS., Vit., B. IX, fol 105 (114); *L.P.*, IV(ii), 3110-11.

3 *Cal. S.P. Milan*, 771; see also *L.P.*, IV(ii), 2891. Russell had criticized Francis's abilities and industry in letters to Wolsey and Henry as early as 1524. See BL, Cotton MSS., Vit., B. VI, fol. 9; *State Papers*, VI, 259; *L.P.*, IV(i), 124, 155.

4 *L.P.*, IV(ii), 3001, 3065-66, 3110; *State Papers*, VI, 578. Russell was designated a knight of the body in a grant for ecclesiastical patronage on 16 June; *L.P.*, IV(ii), 3213(16).

chose him to travel again to Italy and lend assistance to papal allies, but no details about this mission survive if, in fact, it occurred.[1]

Russell's career was quietly progressing. In Rome, he had been very much in the centre of action, even influencing the course of events and earning the trust and good will of his associates there.[2] Now with Henry involved in domestic matters of state, Russell's diplomatic responsibilities yielded to new administrative duties. In the critical years after 1529, from his position in the privy chamber, he witnessed Wolsey's fall, the divorce proceedings, and the rise of Cromwell. At court regularly, comfortable in his relationship with Henry, he was shrewd enough and, at forty-three, still young enough to take advantage of the opportunities which were to open in the new decade.

Russell frequently acted as an intermediary between Henry and Wolsey during the years 1528 and 1529 and in the process seems to have retained the confidence of both men. Sir Thomas Heneage, formerly a member of Wolsey's household and now in the king's privy chamber, was more prominent than Russell in performing the same role.[3] Henry found it convenient not only to assign Russell secretarial tasks but also to use Russell's friendship with Wolsey for his own purpose. For example, in July 1528 the king was angry about a minor matter; Wolsey and Anne Boleyn had quarrelled over the nomination of an abbess for the convent of Wilton. Although Henry supported Anne, Wolsey had ignored her wishes in making the appointment. Anne in turn goaded the king into writing a long, harsh reprimand. Yet Henry hesitated and, before sending the letter, read its contents to both Russell and Heneage that they might help him gauge Wolsey's reaction.[4] Later, in the autumn of 1529, Henry sent Russell as an emissary to Wolsey on a secret midnight visit to reassure the cardinal of the king's support.[5]

Russell and Wolsey shared a mutual affection derived from earlier years when Wolsey had directed Russell's diplomatic missions on the

1   See *L.P.,* IV(ii) 3691, 3710-11, 3713, 3783.

2   See e.g., *ibid.,* 2870, 3077(iii).

3   Starkey, 'The King's Privy Chamber', pp. 317-20. Starkey suggests that Wolsey used politically reliable members of the privy chamber to assume secretarial tasks. See BL, Cotton MSS., Vesp., F. XIII, fol. 254; *State Papers,* I, 301-2; *L.P.,* IV(ii) 4428, 4562, 4799.

4   *State Papers,* I, 316; Paul Friedmann, *Anne Boleyn: A Chapter of English History, 1527-1536* (London, 1884), I, 73-77.

5   George Cavendish, *The Life and Death of Cardinal Wolsey,* ed. Richard S. Sylvester (London, 1959), pp.110-12; *State Papers,* I, 348-49.

continent and, since that time, Russell stood in the cardinal's political debt. Wolsey now included Russell's name when in January 1530 he asked that certain fees and annuities be awarded his friends and servants. He may have hoped to buy new advocates at court with this list but could already depend upon Russell's sympathy and concern.[1] As early as July 1529, Russell had written and urged him good cheer while promising that the king would soon behave in his old, generous manner. Even when this optimistic prophecy failed to materialize, Russell remained solicitious. In February 1530 he earned Anne Boleyn's displeasure by promoting Wolsey's cause in the king's presence. He later approached Thomas Cromwell, still in Wolsey's employ, and asked him to forward a letter to the cardinal: 'I wold his grace shuld not thinke I had forgotten hym'.[2]

Russell's kindness was not unique among Henry's courtiers. Among others, Sir William Paulet, Wolsey's steward, now Russell's colleague in the king's household, also befriended the cardinal. Paulet and Russell were good friends and their careers were to have much in common. Both men were enterprising and ambitious figures in their own right, and neither allowed his friendship with Wolsey to threaten his own position with the king. Nonetheless, their kindness towards Wolsey revealed that compassion and moderation were possible even in an age usually characterized as simply ruthless.[3]

Unfortunately Russell left no record of his thoughts as first the divorce and then the Reformation raised serious intellectual issues within England. It is unlikely that he would have objected to the initial break with Rome on either theoretical or doctrinaire grounds. His recent experiences with Pope Clement could only have reinforced his acceptance of the popular premise that the vicar of Christ was too often a temporal ruler acting in self-interest. Even if private reservations did exist, we cannot know them. Matters of religion he saw as matters of state, and in such issues Russell remained the king's faithful supporter; he understood loyalty as the first prerequisite for success in Tudor politics.

---

[1] *L.P.,* IV(iii), 6181; J.S. Brewer, *The Reign of Henry VIII from his Accession to the Death of Wolsey,* ed. James Gardiner (London, 1884), II, 398-99. Russell received a lifetime annuity of £20 although Wolsey told Cromwell he would have preferred £40.

[2] *L.P.,* IV(iii), 4556; *Cal. S.P. Spain,* IV(i), 257; *L.P.,* IV(i), 6199, 6420.

[3] See Jane Schwartz, 'Practisers in Princes' Causes, Tudor Privy Councillors from 1540 to 1558', unpublished dissertation, Yale University, 1951, p. 239 and Thomson, *Two Centuries of Family History,* p. 193. Cf. also Dickens' remarks on Cromwell's behaviour; A.G. Dickens, *Thomas Cromwell and the English Reformation* (London, 1959), p. 34.

But loyalty notwithstanding, Russell seems to have had few illusions about the king's second wife. He did not like Anne Boleyn, and she was one of the few acquaintances with whom he did not remain on happy terms. The friction between them perhaps began when Russell befriended Wolsey, no friend to Anne. After he publicly defended Wolsey in February 1530, Anne refused to speak to Russell for at least a month.[1] So far as we know, Russell never expressed his personal feelings while Anne remained a power at court, but his restraint disappeared when Henry took Jane Seymour as his third wife in 1536. Writing to Lord Lisle, Russell curtly observed that the 'kyng hath come out of hell into heaven for the gentellness of this and the cursidness and unhappyness in the other'.[2]

Anne Boleyn's influence may have temporarily slowed Russell's progress at court. In 1529 Henry had recalled him *en route* on a mission to the French king to sit instead for Buckinghamshire in the Reformation Parliament.[3] But during the early 1530s, Russell's responsibilities were not impressive and at times must have seemed painfully trivial. One of his major preoccupations in 1532, for instance, centred on the maintenance of Moor Park in Hertfordshire. While Cromwell pondered major Reformation legislation, Russell busily argued with him about the park. Russell complained regularly that his daily fee of 4d. was inadequate for the upkeep of Moor, that if the king were to hunt there with any success a new fence was needed to retain the deer. When additional funds did not arrive despite his grumblings, Russell blamed Cromwell for the delay. The business dragged on through a series of exasperated letters and was resolved only when Lady Russell personally confronted Cromwell.[4]

---

1 *Cal. S.P. Spain*, IV(i), 257. The marriage-wardship dispute involving Russell's stepdaughter also fed their hostility. Anne supported the claims of Thomas Cheyney; *L.P.*, IV(ii), 4456.

2 PRO, S.P. 3/7, fol. 28; *L.P.*, X, 1047. John Wiffen incorrectly dates this letter as 1533, thereby assuming its criticism to be for Queen Catherine. (Wiffen, *Historical Memoirs*, I, 320). In fact, Wiffen's entire treatment of the Boleyn-Russell relationship is filled with inaccuracies, for he confuses Russell with Paulet. Cf. Agnes Strickland, *Lives of the Queens of England* (London, 1890), II, 276 and *L.P.*, X, 1134(4). Strickland quotes Russell making other critical remarks: 'the better Anne Boleyn was apparelled the worse she looked . . .'. The manuscript, however, is too far mutilated to make it clear which queen Russell had in mind.

3 History of Parliament Trust; *L.P.*, IV(iii), 5535, 5541, 6043(2). The History of Parliament Trust notes that Russell may have sat for a Dorset borough in an earlier Parliament and probably sat in the Parliament of 1536. He had also been nominated sheriff for Somerset and Dorset in 1528; Fuller, *Worthies of England*, (I), 288.

4 *L.P.*, IV(iii), 6751(12); V, 976; VI, 401, 426; V, 1285, p. 558; Thomson,

Such episodes may have frustrated Russell, but they did not drive him to leave the court permanently and seek alternative responsibilities. In October 1532 he was among the royal party that landed at Calais When Henry met for the second time with the king of France. Russell spent a fair amount of time in northen France that year, surveying the English holdings and fortifications.[1] Then in 1533 he had the chance to become deputy-governor of Calais — to remain on the continent and use Calais as a base to further his career. He rejected the offer.

The job at Calais went instead to Arthur Plantagenet, Viscount Lisle. Lisle and Russell knew each other well since their careers had overlapped for decades. In fact, in 1533 Russell knew and liked Lisle well enough to give him a bit of advice. Having himself rejected the governorship of Calais, Russell suggested that Lisle do the same. But Lisle ignored the counsel, only to see his career stagnate; his years in Calais did not turn out happily. Rather inept as an administrator, extravagant and often in debt, Lisle was subsequently forced to turn to friends at court for help, many of them, like Russell, useful figures within the privy chamber. By the mid-1530s, Russell was the one able to exert influence and dispense favours while Lisle was in a sense stranded beyond the Channel. Perhaps because Russell remembered his unhappy years at Tournai, he made the right decision in 1533. Later, in 1539, he would tell a mutual friend that Lisle had made a mistake, that affairs would have turned out more profitable for him had he remained in England.[2]

The Calais incident suggests Russell's shrewdness and his methods. Lacking an impressive office, he still chose to stay at court, close to the centre of power. He used his proximity to the king to good advantage. Sensitive to Henry's moods and behaviour, the courtier-politician knew when to flatter, when to indulge his monarch.[3] By the mid-1530s, figures like Reginald Pole, Lord Darcy, and Lisle recognized that Russell enjoyed an unusually good relationship with Henry.[4] Nor did Russell neglect Thomas Cromwell, the king's new chief

---

*Two Centuries of Family History*, p. 151. Series of letters in *L.P.,* VI concerning Moor Park are incorrectly dated as 1533.

1 Nichols, *Chronicle concerning Calais,* pp. 42-43; *L.P.,* V, 1705.

2 *L.P.,* VI, 300(21); IV(iii),6456; XIV(ii), 105; M.L. Bush, 'The Lisle-Seymour Land Disputes', *Historical Journal* 9 (1966), 258-60.

3 See e.g., PRO, S.P. 3/7, fol. 28; *L.P.,* X, 1047.

4 *Cal. S.P. Venice,* V, 575; *L.P.,* XI, 1086, p. 437; X, 952. See also *L.P.,* IV(iii), 6456; VI, 1044. For the gifts and offices which Henry granted Russell during this period, see *L.P.,* IV(ii), 3991(28), 4687(28); IV(iii), 6751(12); VI, 32; VIII, 149(21).

minister. Contemporaries as well as historians have considered Russell one of Cromwell's circle, and the two men were on good terms throughout Cromwell's ascendancy[1]. The quarrel in 1532 concerning Moor Park was a passing affair, leaving no legacy of bitterness.

If Russell appears distant from the crucial decisions associated with the early stages of the Reformation, events finally caught up with his career in 1536. Even before Anne Boleyn's fall, he may have been a member of the king's Council. The fall of the Boleyn party in May created new and promising vacuums of power. In June, however, he risked royal displeasure by advocating Lady Mary as heir apparent. Although some of those associated with Mary, including the Marquis of Exeter, were barred from court, Russell remained unscathed[2]. Within a few months time, a new concern demanded attention: the Pilgrimage of Grace emerged as a rebellion threatening the existence of the Tudor state, absorbing the energy of Henrician officials of all degree and rank. The Pilgrimage marked a major advance for Russell, who impressed the king and Cromwell sufficiently to ensure his inclusion in the newly reorganized Privy Council.

Like so many of his colleagues, Russell could support, first, Henry's religious legislation, then the Reformation under Edward and, finally, Catholicism under Mary, all in the interests of political stability. His Erastianism was in the end a matter of principle, the natural corollary to his dread of civil war. In fact, his principles and his pragmatism, his Erastianism and self-interest, worked together, a perfect marriage, creating in turn his strong loyalty to the throne. The rebellion of 1536, like later uprisings in 1549 and 1553, jeopardized his world and its values, and in each case he was determined to crush the traitors.

Henry naturally depended upon members of the nobility to suppress the Pilgrimage, but Russell was one of several household figures or 'new men' upon whom the king also relied. For his chief commander,

---

1 See G.R. Elton, 'Thomas Cromwell's Decline and Fall', *Cambridge Historical Journal* 10 (1951), 151. The Elizabethan writer John Foxe went so far as to claim that Cromwell saved Russell's life in 1525 and that Russell reciprocated by recommending Cromwell to the king in 1529. But such an early and auspicious origin to their friendship cannot be substantiated. Cf. John Foxe, *Acts and Monuments*, ed. Stephen Reed Catley (London, 1838), II, 419, V, 366-67 and Roger B. Merrimann, *Life and Letters of Thomas Cromwell* (Oxford, 1902), I, 25, 75.

2 See *L.P.*, X, 1134, 1150 and E.W. Ives, 'Faction at the Court of Henry VIII: the Fall of Anne Boleyn', *History* 57 (June 1972), 176. Others in the privy chamber also escaped unharmed.

Henry initially chose the Duke of Suffolk[1] Fought for different reasons in different areas, the rebellion had begun on 1 October in Lincolnshire. By 10 October, the Earls of Shrewsbury, Rutland, and Huntingdon assembled on behalf of the king at Nottingham. Russell and Sir William Parr led a small force at Stamford, where eventually a large proportion of all the king's troops gathered under the combined leadership of Suffolk, Russell, Parr, and Bryan. Also present at Stamford were Sir William Fitzwilliam, the lord high admiral, and Richard Cromwell, nephew of Thomas. The government claimed to have raised an army of 100,000 men. By 17 October, Suffolk, Fitzwilliam, and Russell had entered the town of Lincoln and a day later suppressed the Lincolnshire uprising.[2]

Already, however, the revolt had spread. The Commons of East Riding had reached the town of York and, within a few days, they held Pontefract, Barnard Castle, Durham, and Lancaster. The king, now clearly worried, felt compelled to turn to the Duke of Norfolk despite his suspect religious convictions. Russell sat on Norfolk's council when in late October the duke met for the first time with the rebels at Doncaster. On 8 November, Suffolk dispatched Russell, Bryan, and Richard Cromwell with a force of 700 men to occupy and defend the town of Newark, not an easy task as they later discovered. Meanwhile Suffolk remained at Lincoln until the king ordered him, Russell, and Sir Anthony Browne to join Norfolk at Doncaster in mid-November.[3]

Russell was a cautious, careful man, never the type to rush after glory before carefully weighing risk and dangers. But traits helpful in a civilian career can inhibit the effectiveness of a soldier; caution is not necessarily an advantage in battle. For a time in late October, Russell was disturbed as rumours reached him of the king's displeasure. Henry was allegedly angry over 'slackness', thinking Russell and the others had not advanced quickly enough from Stamford with their troops. When informed that the rumours were ill-founded and that Henry was satisfied with his service, Russell felt relief. His troops, he explained to Cromwell, had tarried only long enough to be supplied with harness,

---

[1] *L.P.*, XI, 536, 576, 656; Madeleine and Ruth Dodds, *The Pilgrimage of Grace 1536-1537 and the Exeter Conspiracy of 1538* (Cambridge, 1915), I, 119-23. For recent interpretations of the Pilgrimage, see G.R. Elton, *Reform and Reformation: England, 1509-1558* (Cambridge, Mass., 1977), pp. 260-73; C.S.F. Davies, 'The Pilgrimage of Grace Reconsidered', *Past and Present,* no. 41 (December 1968), 54-76; M.E. James, 'Obedience in Henrician England: The Lincolnshire Rebellion in 1536', *Past and Present,* no. 48 (August 1970), 3-78.

[2] *L.P.*, XI, 644, 621, 615, 658, 756.

[3] *Ibid.*, 766, 768, 902, 1016, 1103.

weapons, and money. Once they were properly equipped no time had been lost. In 1536, at least, no lasting repercussions ensued; the incident over 'slackness' passed. Suffolk and Fitzwilliam, writing on 20 October, confirmed that Russell, Bryan and Parr lacked men, ordinance, and money. Russell assured Cromwell that he would rather die than have the king think ill of him, but he did not need to employ histrionics. Henry continued to give Russell important assignments and had not lost confidence in him.[1]

Russell's responsibilities went beyond strictly military matters. First at Lincoln and then at Doncaster, he sat on an executive council that made administrative decisions, corresponded with the king, and dealt with prisoners.[2] At Newark he worried about the defence of the castle and the state of the fords which the king's forces would cross.[3] By December he also served as emissary between the king in London and Norfolk and Shrewsbury in Doncaster.[4]

The rebels at this point were meeting in their council at Pontefract to refine their demands and map general strategy. On 2 December Russell left London with Henry's instructions on how to handle the situation. Entrusted with a general royal pardon, Russell was to be Henry's agent and deal directly with Robert Aske and Thomas Lord Darcy, two leaders of the revolt. Henry ordered both Russell and Shrewsbury to act secretly and exclude other members of the executive council from their negotiations with these rebels.[5] Writing to Norfolk, the king explained that Russell should hold onto the pardon and follow directions 'We have with our oune mouth, declared unto him'. The king hoped the rebels would accept a limited pardon. If necessary, Norfolk might agree to a general pardon and even promise a free parliament, but he should delay a week, arrange a temporary truce, and pretend to await the arrival of the general pardon from London.[6] The king thought this deception would gain time and strengthen the government position. Neither Norfolk, Russell, nor their colleagues followed the king's command, however. Norfolk saw no value in delay, and Russell delivered a full and free pardon to the rebels immediately.

---

1 *Ibid.*, 866, 808. Copy of Russell's letter in Bedford Office, Papers of the First Earl, 5.

2 *L.P.*, XI, 672, 756. 902.

3 *Ibid.*, 1087, 1094, 1103.

4 *Ibid.*, 1225, 1227.

5 *Ibid.*, 1225.

6 *State Papers*, I, 514-16; *L.P.*, XI, 1227.

Upon learning the truth, Henry was angry enough to have a letter of rebuke drafted although apparently never sent. Fortunately for Russell and the others, the affair turned out well. Despite his initial displeasure, Henry did not publicly disavow the pardon but, nevertheless, disavowed its spirit, using the opportunity to deceive and eventually capture an unsuspecting Aske.[1]

The impact of his activities on Henry's behalf during the Pilgrimage accelerated Russell's career at court. Most important, his own relationship with Henry gained a stronger foundation and a new dimension, for the king himself directed Russell's assignment and supervised military matters. All in all, it had been a profitable year for Russell. The Boleyns' fall and accompanying privy chamber politics had left him firmly established with both Cromwell and Henry. The revolt gave him a new prominence which king and minister were willing to continue as the military danger declined. Russell's success as courtier, his years of loyal, dependable service, the goodwill which he had carefully nurtured at court — all now brought their reward. Henceforth he was to make his mark as Privy Councillor.

---

[1] *L.P.*, XI, 1271; Dodds, *The Pilgrimage of Grace,* II, 226. For Russell's role in the aftermath of the rebellion, see *L.P.*, XI, 1410; XII(i), 734(1), 1227(4).

# 2

## PATRONAGE AND FRIENDSHIP

Russell won distinction both as a Privy Councillor after 1536 and as one of Henry's new nobles after 1539. His offices and honours, however, tell only part of the story, the public side of his success. Just as significant were the unofficial activities Russell pursued at court: the friendships and relationships which he cultivated, the patronage which he collected and distributed. These 'connections' deserve attention in their own right. They reflect the very nature of the Tudor system, reveal Russell's mode of operaton, and underlie his public career. Hard work and loyalty were essential but not sufficient ingredients for success.

The official distinctions and appointments came on a number of fronts. It is not possible to pinpoint when Russell entered the king's Council, but he was a member after Cromwell's reorganization in late 1536. Russell did not initially participate in its deliberations since he served the king on the battlefield during the Pilgrimage of Grace. On 30 January 1537, however, he signed his first letter as a member of the reorganized Council and subsequently attended its sessions regularly whenever he was at court. Yet his duties as councillor changed neither his basic pattern of behaviour nor his basic concept of government. Like most of his colleagues, he specialized neither as an administrator nor as a bureaucrat but continued to perform a variety of functions at court and on the battlefield. Even while being initiated into the business of the Privy Council, he assumed new responsibilities in the king's household. His friend, Sir William Paulet, had been comptroller, an administrative post concerned with provisioning the court, second in the household only to the lord steward and treasurer. Russell inherited the office in 1537 when Paulet was promoted and named treasurer.[2]

In the spring of 1539, the Russells moved to a new house in London on the Strand, a symbol of their growing prominence.[3] Russell's

---

1   See *L.P.*, XII(i), 291 and G.R. Elton, *The Tudor Revolution in Government: Administrative Changes in the Reign of Henry VIII* (Cambridge, 1953), pp. 317-42.

2   Russell served as comptroller for less than two years. His account book, in which he supervised daily expenditures at court, survives. See PRO E 101/422/10 and Thomson, *Two Centuries of Family History*, p. 158.

3   *L.P.*, XIV(i), 867 (cap. 26).

unobtrusive but steady accumulation of property and royal grants was beginning to pay off. He was worth £551.19s.4d. by June 1539.[1] The figure includes fees, annuities, Anne's jointure (£183) and, of course, landed property (£305.19s.4d.). The lands had come primarily from inheritance (£33), marriage (£120.13s.4d), and grants (£115.10s.4d.). Only a minimal amount had been leased or purchased (£37.2s.8d.). It was an income in which Russell could take pride, but it still represented a modest sum compared to what was to come. In July 1539, after a career spanning thirty years, his wealth was doubled.

The events of 1539 dramatically changed his position and in more ways than one made Russell a new man. Giving up the office of comptroller, he received a barony in March and then the highest of honours, installation as Knight of the Garter.[2] He became lord president of the Council of the West, an office which Cromwell created in April.[3] In July the crown appointed him steward of the duchy of Cornwall and lord warden of the stannaries, important positions in the west.[4] He was also kept busy throughout the spring and summer on a commission for maintaining coastal defence in the west. Underlying all the new honours and offices was an impressive gift of lands, drawn primarily from the former monastery of Tavistock, some thirty thousand acres worth £648.12s. after the subtraction of reserved rents.[6]

Seen in its larger context, Russell's elevation is another instance of Henry VIII's creation of a new nobility to strengthen his dynasty. The king promoted and rewarded a group of men whose loyalty he needed and trusted. Russell was one of twelve such peers created during the years 1539-1547. All told, there were twenty-five new nobles during

1  PRO, E 315/418, corrected in Joyce Youngs, *Devon Monastic Lands: Calendar of Particulars for Grants, 1536-1558,* Devon and Cornwall Record Society, New Series, I (Torquay, 1955), p. 5, note 1. Russell had received grants worth over £70 from the king during the spring of 1538. Some of these lands, valued at £33 *per annum,* had originally been granted to Sir Richard Jerningham and were still in the possession of Lady Russell. They could now pass directly to Russell's own heir. *L.P.,* XIII(i), 115(37-39): 1309(8). All values derived from PRO, E 315/418. Russell also received £500 from the king, paid in instalments in February and March of 1539. This unusually large sum came out of household expenses and in all probability stemmed from Russell's obligations as comptroller. See *L.P.,* XIV(ii), 781 (f.59), (f.61b).

2  *L.P.,* XIV(i), 651(18), 833, 979.

3  *Ibid.,* 904(12).

4  *Ibid.,* 1354(12).

5  *Ibid.,* 398, 685.

6  *Ibid.,* 1354(13).

Henry's reign. The year 1539 was especially bountiful because of the sudden availability of monastic lands. Sir William Paulet and Sir William Parr were also made barons in March.[1] Paulet, henceforth Lord St John, had long been Russell's companion at court while Parr, a younger man, had made his mark during the Pilgrimage of Grace. In addition, long-time associates accompanied Russell at his installation as Knight of the Garter – Sir Thomas Cheyney and Sir William Kingston, now respectively the treasurer and comptroller of the household.[2]

The king expected his nobles not only to serve his interests at Westminister but also to ensure tranquillity in their home countries. In this sense he intended Russell's elevation to solve a special problem. A power vacuum had existed in the west since the 1538 attainder and execution of Henry Courtenay, Marquis of Exeter. Henry himself chose Russell to fill the gap.[3] As Russell's new offices indicated, the transformation of his status, influence, and wealth was all meant to make the 'west partes' more secure. His career would henceforth reflect a new but permanent association with the western counties, lasting not only throughout the remainder of his lifetime but also maintained by his son, the second Earl of Bedford.

Henry was thus Russell's chief patron, his most important 'connection'. Russell never depended upon a particular office as much as he relied upon Henry's trust and confidence to protect and enhance his own political position. Still a gentleman of the privy chamber, he enjoyed regular access to the king, often on a daily basis. Commenting on the king's excellent spirits in July of 1537, Russell could remark that Henry 'useth himself more like a good fellow than like a king among us that be here'.[4] And in the spring of 1538, Castillon, the French ambassador at the English court, referred to the close relationship which existed between the king and his councillor.[5]

Russell's ability to cultivate and maintain Henry's favour and

---

1    *Ibid.,* 651(19-20). See Wallace MacCaffrey, 'England: The Crown and the New Aristocracy, 1540-1600' *Past and Present,* no. 30 (April 1965), 55.

2    *L.P.,* XIV(i), 979. Cheyney has been named with Russell in the Eltham Ordinances; Kingston's career, like Russell's, stretched back to the position of usher at the funeral of Henry VII. *L.P.,* IV(i), 1939(4); I(i), 20 (f. 120).

3 ·  PRO, S.P. 1/44, fols, 116 and 160; *L.P.,* XIV(i), 529 and 590.

4    *L.P.,* XII(ii), 242.

5    M. Jean Kulak, ed., *Correspondence politique MM. de Castillon et de Marillac, ambassadeurs de France en Angleterre (1537-1542)* (Paris, 1885), 60; also *L.P.,* XIII(i), 994. After the death of Jane Seymour, Russell and his wife were among those granted jewels belonging to the late queen. *L.P.,* XII(ii), 973(ii and v).

goodwill rested largely on his own powers of perception and his understanding of Henry's nature. After Henry's death, testifying at a treason trial in 1549, Russell spoke of the one trait he saw as characteristic of the Tudor monarchs – their sense of insecurity. Russell claimed that Henry VIII, like his father and probably like his son, 'was a prynce of moche wisdome and knowledge yet he was veary suspicious and much given to suspicion. . . .'[1] Perceptive enough to recognize this psychological reality, Russell was able to satisfy the king's needs by always acting the loyal and reliable servant. This was not a difficult formula to follow: the king did not demand obsequious behaviour. As Thomas, Lord Darcy claimed, Russell was among those who 'dare and wyll speke to the King the tryth . . .'[2] Henry tolerated such independence precisely because Russell had demonstrated his loyalty and reliability.

Russell's unobtrusiveness served him well with respect to Henry's moods and irritability, especially the king's notorious tendency to turn on trusted servants in a fit of anger and discard them. Russell's intellect and personality together helped him survive and eventually thrive at Henry's court. More creative, imaginative and assertive minds undoubtedly left more of a mark upon the Tudor state, but in the end such men were likely to be authors of their own undoing. They had policies and ideas to press upon the king, ideas which made them vulnerable and could be the excuse for acts of attainder. Russell's intelligence was of a different sort. During Henry's reign he carefully avoided the trap of factional politics. He was concerned with appraising and serving his colleagues and superiors, with gaining their gratitude and confidence rather than advocating policies of state.[3]

An incident from 1543 provides further evidence of his insight into Henry's temperament. The conservative faction in the Privy Council, led by Norfolk and Bishop Gardiner, turned on Archbishop Cranmer and nearly achieved his downfall. When they informed Henry that Cranmer was a heretic, the king agreed that the Council confront the archbishop with their charge. But then Henry changed his mind, if he had ever been serious, and at the last moment, before the Council met, he gave Cranmer a ring as a sign of affection and protection. The king's reversal shocked most of the councillors, but not Lord Russell, who angrily reminded his colleagues that he had predicted this

1  PRO, S.P. 10/6, fol. 44.
2  PRO, S.P. 1/111, fol. 142; *L.P.*, XI, 1086, p. 437.
3  Cf. A. L. Rowse, *Tudor Cornwall,* 2nd ed. (London, 1969), pp. 239-40.

outcome. He knew 'right well' that Henry would never permit Cranmer 'such a blemish as to be imprisoned, unless it were for high treason'.[1]

Russell had avoided all contact with the conspirators. Perhaps he was reluctant to become involved since he liked Cranmer and disliked faction. His outburst in Council suggests an additional explanation, namely that he recognized the special relationship between the king and his archbishop, a bond firm enough to survive either difference of opinion or intrigue at court. This relationship was not dissimilar to Russell's own relationship with the king. All the Henricians were, of course, dependent upon the king's favour, but Cranmer and Russell were unique in relying so exclusively upon the king. Each, a few years older than Henry, managed to establish a successful rapport with the king. Neither man used patronage or intrigue as an alternative, independent source of power. And the king, for his part, remained faithful to each of them.

Although Russell may have understood Henry's needs, the king made the final choice, allowed the relationship to continue, and distributed the rewards. The relationship during the 1540s became more than a conventional one. On several occasions it verged on a genuine friendship, at least as much of a friendship as a Tudor despot might experience. The bond remained firm even through times of tension such as the summer of 1544, when Russell criticized Henry's military policy.[2] In 1545 the Venetian ambassador singled out Lord Russell as an impressive figure at court. Not only did he hold a position of authority within the Privy Council, but he also served as a regular dining and conversational companion for the king.[3] Both men were growing old together; Russell at sixty was destined to survive another decade while Henry at fifty-four was sick and ageing beyond his time. During the king's final years, Russell was not as powerful a figure as Edward Seymour, William Paget, or John Dudley. Yet he contained as a favourite, and when Henry discussed the provisions of his will with some of his councillors, he included Russell. The will itself was generous toward Russell, insuring his prominence in the next reign.[4] Even in death Henry proved to be Russell's friend and patron.

---

1 Quoted in John Strype, *Memorials of the Most Reverend Father in God, Thomas Cranmer* . . . (Oxford, 1840), I, 180. See also 165.

2 See below, p. 47-48.

3 *Cal. S.P. Ven.*, VI(iii), Appendix, 118, p. 1635.

4 John Strype, *Ecclesiastical Memorials Relating Chiefly to Religion and the Reformation* . . . (Oxford, 1822), III(i), 455; *L.P.*, XXI(ii), 634.

With his colleagues at court, Russell maintained informal, friendly ties, always limited by political realities. His associates generally liked him, and he collected few enemies during his lifetime. Perhaps his closest and longest friendship was with St John (later the Marquis of Winchester), whom he ultimately named as an executor of his will.[1] Even men who did not themselves get along — for example, Sir Thomas Wyatt the Elder and Edmund Bonner, Bishop of London — were agreed in their affection for Russell.[2] Russell's frankness kept him from developing a bland or fawning personality, and like so many Henricians, he had a sharp temper which he sometimes indulged. But despite occasional harsh words, the final impression is one of goodwill between Russell and his colleagues.

Russell was especially careful to maintain friendship with Thomas Cromwell, his most important benefactor after the king himself. Seeking help for a relative, servant, or friend, Russell often approached the king's secretary and usually went away satisfied. Sometimes he used Cromwell as a convenient conduit to channel messages to the king. While sick and absent from court for a prolonged period in the summer of 1538, Russell begged Cromwell to make his excuses to the king.[3] For his part, Russell was glad to extend favours and do some good for the secretary. When Cromwell himself had been absent from court in July of 1537, one of his men, Sir Ralph Sadler, provoked Henry's anger. Russell first made excuses for Sadler and then wrote to Cromwell to suggest how Henry might best be appeased.[4]

Such a friendship was only natural during the 1530s when men at court wooed the secretary as a powerful figure close to the throne. A different atmosphere prevailed, however, once Henry lost confidence in his chief minister and placed him under arrest in June 1540. The French Ambassador Marillac then predicted that Cromwell could count only Russell and Archbishop Cranmer as real friends on the Privy Council and that even they would give the secretary no help or comfort. Cranmer 'dare not open his mouth' whereas Russell had 'long learned to bend to all winds . . . .'[5]

---

1   F. 5 Ketchyn; Thomson, *Two Centuries of Family History*, p. 193.

2   See Inner Temple Library, Petyt MS. 538, vol. 43, fols. 3, 9 and Loades, *The Papers of George Wyatt Esquire*, p. 28.

3   *L.P.*, XIII(ii), 673. See also, VII, 1084, 1223: XI, 225.

4   *Ibid.*, XII(ii), 242. See Arthur Joseph Slavin, *Politics and Profit: A Study of Sir Ralph Sadler 1507-1547* (Cambridge, Mass., 1966), p. 33.

5   Kaulek, *Correspondence politique*, pp. 189-94 or *L.P.*, XV, 767.

Marillac was wrong about Cranmer, who alone among the Privy Councillors wrote to the king on Cromwell's behalf.[1] But he was right about Russell, whose sympathy remained tacit. Although at hand to witness Cromwell's misfortune, Russell expressed none of the concern that he had shown for Wolsey in similar circumstances ten years earlier. In fact as a prominent councillor, he was expected to participate in the proceedings against the secretary. He went with Norfolk to examine Cromwell in the Tower and eventually, like most of the councillors, provided the king with a hostile deposition.[2] Norfolk hated Cromwell, a reaction easily understood. As a member of the old nobility, he resented the secretary's power. Russell's stance reflected political realities just as obvious as those motivating Norfolk. Loyalty was owed to the king, who after all, had the right and the duty to decide the fate of his own servants. If Russell had been more vocal in his support of Wolsey a decade earlier, the cardinal's disgrace had followed a pattern different from that which Cromwell's followed. Wolsey's death may have been hastened by his political downfall, but it was, nevertheless, a natural death. Cromwell, however, was under arrest and clearly marked for execution. Intervention in this instance would be intervention against a royal decision already made explicit.

Friendship and connection led to patronage, which in turn could change hands a number of times before reaching its final recipient. One first collected favours and grants and then redistributed a fair share to friends, clients, and relatives while receiving in exchange either gratuities or at the very least gratitude and influence. In this sense, patronage was both a reflection and source of power, a sign of prestige among the governing elite. For the historian, patronage provides its own riches, a means of investigating a man's friends, politics, or even his religious preference. In Russell's case, intercessions for friends and relatives became noticeable after 1529 as his diplomatic missions abroad were curtailed and he found himself in a favourable position at court. As one would expect, he acted on behalf of acquaintances, relatives, favourite clerics and, finally, those gentry whose cooperation was a prerequisite for political stability in the west. Since he avoided faction, however, he handed out favours on a random basis, never intending to create a party at court or a personal following.

A sample of Russell's activities reveals how diverse and far-flung his friends were. Early in the 1530s, for example, he had connections

---

1   *L.P.*, XV, 770; Elton, 'Thomas Cromwell's Decline and Fall', pp. 151-52.

2   Gilbert Burnet, *The History of the Reformation of the Church of England*, ed. Nicholas Pocock (Oxford, 1865), I, 447-48; IV, 424.

with English travellers and humanists in northern Italy, a tie perhaps begun during his own travels in the 1520s. Thomas Winter, Wolsey's illegitimate son, wrote from Padua in 1533 to express his gratitude and obligation for services Russell had rendered. Russell's friendship with the late cardinal probably motivated his kindness in this case. Studying in Italy, Winter came into contact with many of Russell's acquaintances there. The Bishop of Verona, formerly a papal datary, was glad to hear of Russell's welfare.[1] Reginald Pole, leader of the English humanist circle in Italy, also considered himself one of Russell's friends. In 1530 or 1531, before he broke publicly with the king, Pole asked Russell to present Henry with some of his writing on the divorce issue. He expressed fear lest Russell incur the king's anger, but Russell assured Pole, 'knowing me as he did — he would present the writing let happen whatever pleased God'.[2]

As already noted, another beneficiary of Russell's influence during the 1530s was Viscount Lisle, deputy governor of Calais. No other connection better typified the practice of the age. Lisle's agent in London, John Hussee, handed out gifts to the right people at court while prodding them to act on Lisle's behalf. Although Russell usually proved to be a helpful and willing ally, he nevertheless refused to interfere in 1536 when a land dispute developed between Lisle and Edward Seymour. The explanation for Russell's restraint is not difficult to find: the king had married Seymour's sister. After the death of Queen Jane, Russell again took up his friend's cause.[3] The Lisles and the Russells clearly liked one another. The two wives exchanged recipes, and when Lady Lisle's son, John Basset, visited Chenies, he was entertained there 'most lovingly'.[4] The incident in 1536, however, underlines Russell's care lest friendship conflict with good politics.

As Russell's wealth and authority increased in the 1540s, the favours at his disposal grew in attraction. Under his auspices, his secretary John Gale sat for the Devonshire borough of Totnes in the Parliament of 1545; in 1547 Gale represented Tavistock, a borough in Russell's possession since the grant of 1539. In 1548, Gale became a reversioner clerk of the privy seal, eventually working in the office which Russell himself headed.[5] Likewise, Russell presented his kinsman, William

---

1   *L.P.,* VI, 315. See above, p. 18, n.1.

2   *Cal. S.P. Ven.,* V, 575, p. 244.

3   Bush, 'The Lisle-Seymour Land Disputes', pp. 264-65, 271. Russell, unlike Lisle's other friends, was at least willing to pledge him some money in 1536.

4   *L.P.,* XIII(ii), 431.

5   History of Parliament Trust, courtesy of Professor S.T. Bindoff and *Cal. Pat. Rolls, Edw. VI,* II, 81. See also PRO, S.P. 10/4, fols. 87-88.

Fitzwilliam, to King Edward VI, who appointed him marshal of the king's bench. Fitzwilliam too received the fruits of parliamentary patronage when in 1553 he sat for Peterborough, a borough where Russell served as high steward.[1]

Of course, Russell showed the most persistent solicitude for his son and sole heir, Francis, who began receiving commissions and government appointments in the 1540s while still an adolescent. In 1545 at the age of eighteen, Francis entered Parliament sitting for Buckinghamshire, where the family owned a great deal of land. In two years time, he was named sheriff of Bedfordshire, returned to Parliament, and was created a knight of the bath for Edward's coronation.[2] During Edward's reign, he received stewardships to several parks and manors, all offices surrendered by his father and, during the early stages of Mary's reign, he benefited from his father's protection and good name.[3]

Russell's circle of clients also included a number of clerics. He had been collecting advowsons at least since 1527, and this particular form of patronage naturally increased after 1539 with the redistribution of monastic and even episcopal lands. Yet livings were often already occupied, and the evidence concerning Russell's own appointments is unfortunately too spotty to draw real conclusions. When an advowson does appear in the records, it was either sold for profit or granted to an obscure cleric.[4] On the other hand, Russell did maintain a few highly visible friendships among the clergy. He intervened, for example, in 1534 on behalf of his neighbour John Chambers, abbot of Peterborough, then involved in a dispute before star chamber. Later, as the Dissolution approached, Russell voiced concern for the abbot's fate. He assured Cromwell that Chambers was 'as obbedyent as any of his cote' and kept church goods without embezzling them. When Chambers's house won even a temporary reprieve, Russell expressed gratitude. In 1539 with Dissolution a certainty, he again intervened for his friend, this time to request a pension.[5] His commendations may have ultimately worked to Chambers's advantage; in 1541 the former abbot became the first bishop of the newly created see at Peterborough.[6]

1  History of Parliament Trust.

2  *Ibid., Cal. Pat. Rolls, Edw. VI*, I, 181.

3  *Ibid.*, IV, 145-46. See below, p. 97, n. 3 and p. 98, n. 3.

4  E.g., *ibid.*, I, 4,; George Oliver, *Monasticon Dioecesis Exoniensis* (Exeter, 1846), p. 93.

5  *L.P.*, VII, 791; PRO, S.P. 1/135, fol. 236; *L.P.*, XIV(ii), 419.

6  Bridges, *History and Antiquities of Northamptonshire*, II, 559.

Russell's new acquisition of monastic and bishopric property did not preclude his friendship with the very churchmen deprived of the use of these lands. He remained on good terms with Veysey, Bishop of Exeter, for whose estates he was nominal steward although the crown forced Veysey to alienate much property which ultimately fell under Russell's control. Likewise, after 1539 Lord and Lady Russell sustained a friendship with John Peryn, the former abbot of Tavistock monastery. In addition to the £100 pension granted Peryn upon the Dissolution, Russell provided him with a house, a modest but comfortable residence. The relationship proved mutually profitable, for when the Russells found themselves short of funds, Peryn loaned them money.[1]

Profit, friendship, and patronage also merged in the case of Russell's wards. Records show that Russell purchased eight wardships during his lifetime and, in at least one case, he leased his ward's land. But these purchases often reflected ties of kinship and friendship as much as pure and cold economic realities. His first wardship, purchased in 1537/8 was conditional, subject to the death of the ward's grandfather. The minor in question was John Wyse, no doubt a relative of Russell's mother, Alice Wyse of Syndenham.[2] Similarly, in 1543, Russell paid £66.13s.4d. for the wardship of Robert Sapcote, a relative of his wife.[3] Other wards, John Pollard and Henry Trenchard, were the sons of western associates. Although the Pollard purchase included a profitable lease, sentiment and western politics were also involved. The Pollards had long been active in western politics, and Russell later placed John in Parliament.[4]

Russell acted strictly for personal reasons when he performed favours for friends and relatives. But as the Pollard case indicates, his patronage embraced another significant group, men of the west, gentry and merchants whose goodwill was necessary to ensure political well-being in the western shires. In this case he used his position and

---

1 For Veysey, see below, p. 109, 110-11. For Peryn, see Richard Worth, *Calender of the Tavistock Parish Records* (Plymouth, 1887), pp. 120, 122; Thomson, *Family Background,* p. 198; H.P.R. Finberg, *Tavistock Abbey: A Study in the Social and Economic History of Devon,* 2nd. ed (New York, 1969), p. 270.

2 PRO, Wards 9/149, fol. 104 and Wards 9/151. Russell received an annuity by 1554; *L.P.,* XIX(i), 444(9).

3 PRO, Wards 9/149, fol. 132 and Wards 9/262.

4 PRO, Wards 9/149, fol. 120; Wards 9/187, fol. 33; *L.P.,* XVIII(ii), 241(8); Wards 9/154; Inner Temple Library, Petyt MS. 536, vol. 46, fol. 438; History of Parliament Trust.

influence to reinforce the interests of the dynasty as well as to enhance his personal prestige.

The patronage and favours began as early as 1539 when Russell acquired his Tavistock lands and western offices. He proved willing to extend courtesies, make interventions at court, and distribute some of the offices and appointments at his disposal.[1] As high steward of the duchy of Cornwall, he employed officials himself and influenced royal appointments. As lord warden, he chose staff for stannary courts, bailiffs for stannary districts, and keepers for stannary castles and forests. His influence was clearly at work for Sir Hugh Trevanion, a member of the western gentry, who was named escheator and feodary of the duchy of Cornwall and constable of Launceston Castle shortly after Russell's Tavistock grant.[2] In 1551 just as Russell became earl, Trevanion surrendered his original patent in order to receive a joint grant with his son. That son, significantly, was chief steward for Russell's western estates and a close enough associate to witness Russell's will.[3] Another western man, John Haydon served as escheator of Devon, attorney to the city of Exeter, and under-steward for Henry Courtenay's former lands. Russell, himself steward of the Courtenay holdings, may have endorsed any or all of these appointments, for various incidents link him to Haydon.[4]

Additional duchy officials cannot be identified as the beneficiaries of Russell's patronage. Some owed their positions to Sir Thomas Arundell, receiver general of the duchy, and others the crown itself nominated. Many were the usual western men one would expect to fill such positions. Sir William Godolphin, for instance, served as vice warden and comptroller of the stannary. Although Russell knew the Godolphins and sat with William's father on the Council of the West, Godolphin was a natural appointee in his own right. His family wealth

---

1   Russell successfully intervened for the family of the late Sir Piers Edgcumbe, a member of the Council of the West. *L.P.,* XIV(ii), 371, 455, 494-95; XV, 942(32).

2   *Ibid.,* XIV(ii), 435(32), 435(35).

3   *Cal. Pat. Rolls, Edw. VI,* IV, 8; F. 5 Ketchyn.

4   Russell was named steward of the duchy of Exeter in 1539, a reference to the Courtenay family lands; *L.P.* XIV(i), 1354(12). Haydon entered Lincoln's Inn in 1529, the year in which Russell was made an honorary member. He married a cadet line of the Grenvilles, an important western family friendly with Russell. and purchased property from Russell himself in 1539. In 1558 after Russell's death, he sat for the duchy borough of Denheved (Launceston), susceptible to the Bedford influence. See *Records of the Honorable Society of Lincoln's Inn* (1896), I. 44-45; below p. 106. I am indebted to the History of Parliament Trust for biographical information on Haydon (alias Heydon).

came from tin, and family members, including his father, had long held comparable stannary positions.[1]

Russell's western patronage is most visible not in administrative appointments but in the House of Commons. The whole question of parliamentary patronage will not be settled until the History of Parliament Trust completes its valuable work, but the research already done suggests that John Russell in a casual, unsystematic way actually began the parliamentary patronage usually associated with his son. His offices — steward of the duchy, warden of the stannary and, on occasion, lord lieutenant — and his position as lord of Tavistock borough and western magnate gave him the opportunity to influence selection of MPs.

Again, some connections are certain, others probable. The men who sat for Tavistock certainly did so under Russell's auspices. Some such as Sir Peter Carew (1545), John Gale (1547), and Edward Underhill (March 1553) were family friends or associates. At times, Russell acted for the crown as when in October 1553, Tavistock returned Richard Wilbraham, a courtier and a favourite of Queen Mary. Barnstaple, a borough in north Devon, returned William Gardiner in March 1553 and Sir John Pollard in 1554, both former wards to Lord Russell. Another MP associated with the Russell name, indeed mentioning the family in his will, was Sir Humphrey Cavell, a local man who sat for duchy boroughs in 1553 and 1554. Russell's influence appears especially strong and persistent in Dunheved (Launceston), the most important of all duchy boroughs in the sixteenth century.[2] Moreover, seven Cornish towns, newly enfranchised in 1547, came immediately under Russell's influence, and the History of Parliament Trust suggests that he probably encouraged their enfranchisement.

What is so intriguing and elusive about parliamentary patronage is the many different ways in which western gentry members were connected and related to one another. Not surprisingly, it is often impossible to conclude which was the decisive factor behind any one election. The Grenvilles and the Russells shared influence in the area, knew each other, and had mutual friends.[3] Under such circumstances,

---

1  *L.P.*, IV(ii), 4445(23);   BL, Harl. MS. 6380, fols. 6-7; Duchy of Cornwall Office, Receiver General Accounts.

2  William Cavell, who sat for Dunheved in 1545 and 1547, was cousin to Humphrey Cavell and probably had ties with Russell. A Russell connection was also possible for five of the other seven Dunheved members during the period 1545-1554. All examples of parliamentary influence are derived from the files of the History of Parliament Trust.

3  See *L.P.*, XIV(ii), 105. Lady Grenville was the niece of Lady Lisle; Rowse,

it becomes very difficult to determine who acted for whom. Or consider Robert Walshe, elected for Dunheved in 1554, a friend to both Russell and the Edgcumbe family. Even if Russell was responsible for Walshe's return, he may have done it as a favour for the Edgcumbes. Similar confusion surrounds Lincoln's Inn, where Russell enjoyed honorary membership since 1529.[1] Sir Thomas Arundell also belonged to Lincoln's Inn and, like Russell, wielded parliamentary influence. In fact, in 1545 Arundell supervised parliamentary elections in all the southwest. To decide whether Arundell or Russell acted as patron for another Inn member is accordingly tricky if not impossible. Ultimately all the inter-connections and overlapping influences are in their own way as revealing as the explicit instances of parliamentary nominations. Russell used his patronage in the west to reinforce not disrupt the traditional gentry leadership.

Just as Russell cannot be associated with any one political faction, neither did he consistently favour or befriend men of any one religious preference. A long and important list of historians — Foxe, Strype, Froude, Pollard, and Jordan — have classified Russell as a Protestant or religious Reformer, a label contested by Gladys Scott Thomson.[2] When we look at Russell's collection of friends and the distribution of his patronage, the evidence is at best contradictory, and the Protestant conclusion does not necessarily follow.

Russell certainly included good Protestants among his friends both at court, most notably Cromwell and Cranmer, and outside court as well. Sir Thomay Wyatt the Elder, a friend to Russell since the 1520s, was mourned in death as a Protestant believer. William Fitzwilliam, John Gale, Sir Peter Carew, Sir Edward Rogers, and Edward Underhill, all recipients of Russell's parliamentary patronage, stood firmly in the Protestant camp.[3] Furthermore as the Reformation took hold in England and the decade of the 1540s progressed, Russell's actions themselves often reflected Protestant tendencies or sympathies. He

---

*Tudor Cornwall*, p. 242.

1 See above, p. 39, n. 4.

2 Foxe, *Acts and Monuments*, V, 438-39; Strype, *Memorials of Thomas Cranmer*, I, 108; Wiffen, *Historical Memoirs*, I, 354-55; Froude, 'Cheneys and the House of Russell', p. 368. A.F. Pollard, *England Under Protector Somerset* (London, 1900), pp. 20-21; W. K. Jordan, *Edward VI*, vol. I, *The Young King* (Cambridge, Mass., 1968), 56-57, 128. Contrast Thomson, *Two Centuries of Family History*, pp. 198, 201 and *Family Background*, p. 93. Also Pollard's later work, *The History of England from the Accession of Edward VI to the Death of Elizabeth (1547-1603)* (London, 1919), pp. 3-4.

3 History of Parliament Trust.

acted with complete equanimity when commissioned to try Richard Whiting, abbot of Glastonbury, a steadfast Catholic convicted and executed for treason in 1539.[1] Later in Henry's reign when Gardiner and Norfolk attempted to purge some Protestant courtiers from the privy chamber, Russell opposed their moves.[2] During the reign of Edward VI when ordered to proceed against western rebels protesting the Book of the Common Prayer, Russell brought with him as chaplain Miles Coverdale, a man of deep Protestant convictions.[3]

Yet such evidence is at best circumstantial and, for the most part, is Protestantism by association. A contradictory picture is easy enough to paint using different examples. To argue the Catholic case, one can note that in the mid-1530s Russell also had the trust of Lord Darcy, a leader in the Pilgrimage of Grace.[4] His lack of compassion for the abbot of Glastonbury in 1539 coincided in the very same letter with his concern for the abbot of Peterborough.[5] In 1543 Edmund Bonner, an Henrician bishop not known for Protestant inclinations, saw Russell responsible for his 'honorable preferrment' and thanked him for 'fatherlie grave, and wise frendle counsell'.[6] Another of his close colleagues at court, Sir Anthony Browne, held conservative religious views.[7] Moreover, the restoration of Catholicism under Mary did nothing to impede his career. In contrast to his association with Miles Coverdale during Edward's reign, in Queen Mary's time he was on the best of terms with John Feckenham, abbot of Westminster, a conservative cleric earlier imprisoned for his Catholic views. A good family friend, Feckenham witnessed John Russell's will and later preached at Anne Russell's funeral.[8]

All these ambivalences and contradictions had their own

---

1  BL, Cotton MSS., Cleop., E. IV, fol. 119.

2  Foxe, *Acts and Monuments*, V, 495-96.

3  See Nicholas Pocock, ed., *Troubles Connected with the Prayer Book of 1549*, Camden Society, XXXVII (London, 1884), 7, note b. I would like to thank Professor Conrad Russell for drawing my attention to Coverdale.

4  See above p. 32, n.2.

5  BL, Cotton MSS., Cleop., E. IV, fol. 119.

6  Inner Temple Library, Petyt MS. 538, vol. 47, fol. 3.

7  Browne spoke of the 'special love, favor, and hearty affection' he felt for Russell whom he named as one of the executors of his will. 10 Coode; Schwartz, 'Practisers of Princes' Causes', p. 231.

8  F. 5 Ketchyn; Thomson, *Family Background*, pp. 92-93; *DNB*, IV, 1147. As early as 1550, the Imperial ambassador, Simon Renard, claimed that Russell kept 'the good faith'. Upon Russell's death in 1555, Renard called him 'a good imperialist' who had 'made ample profession of the true faith', *Cal. S.P. Spain*, X 8; XIII, 146.

significance. As his whole career demonstrated, Russell was neither a committed Catholic nor a dedicated Protestant. He was in fact not at all motivated by ideological considerations, in this respect very much resembling colleagues like Richard Rich, William Paget or St John. Their Erastian views reflected their fear of civil war and point to the pragmatism inherent in the English Reformation from its inception. They also draw attention to another equally important characteristic of the English Reformation, the general consensus upon which it rested. During various doctrinal changes, dogma did not divide the English church so much as a broad Erastian tradition united it. Russell and his colleagues, assured of general Christian principles, placed priority upon political stability and unity. Such men, at least during the Henrician period, distributed favours and made friends within all ideological camps.[1]

If Russell's patronage as a whole is reviewed, a consistent picture thus emerges. Kinship, friendship, and patronage reinforced each other. Outside the western interest, he did not work for men of one political faction or party and even in the west acted unobtrusively in co-operation with resident gentry. He created no coherent group of political clients or ideological allies at court. Finally, although willing to help others, he did not let consideration for them undermine his own political or economic power. Russell, rather than his clients, derived the most benefit from the system.

[1] See Conrad Russell, *The Crisis of Parliaments, English History, 1509-1660* (London, 1971), p. 81; Barrett J. Beer, *Northumberland. The Political Career of John Dudley* . . . (Columbus, 1973), pp. 25-27.

# 3

## COUNCILLOR AND CRITIC, 1540-1549

The decade of the 1540s represented the climax of Russell's career in national politics. In July 1540, just one year after the Tavistock grant, King Henry appointed him lord admiral.[1] The promotion came amid the general reshuffling of offices caused by Cromwell's fall and indicates that Russell had impressed the king while supervising coastal defences in the west. His stature increased further when, in December 1542, he became lord privy seal; in 1544 he served as captain of the vanguard in the war against France.[2] He successfully survived the change of regime after Henry's death and, although keeping some distance from the Duke of Somerset, sat on Edward VI's Council. In short, throughout the decade, he remained active and won respect as an important, experienced councillor. Always secure at court, he occasionally used his status as elder councillor to express his independent judgement and opinions, even when those opinions questioned prevailing policy and attitudes.

A Holbein drawing from the 1540s shows Russell as he probably appeared to his contemporaries: a serious and private man with strong features and a full, white beard. Holbein deliberately drew his subject in partial profile, obscuring from full view Russell's right eye, which had been injured and made useless in battle some twenty years earlier.[3] Whatever the hidden psychological effects, Russell minimized his handicap, leaving behind no trace of complaint, just as his colleagues never spoke of the wound. Holbein's drawing reflects the reality: the injury remains subordinate to the portrait's suggestion of a man of perception and purpose.

Many of Russell's official actions reflected military concerns, a theme which predominated at Henry's court by the spring of 1541 and

---

1 *L.P.*, XV, 942(117).

2 *Ibid.*, XVII, 1251(7); XX(i), 621(4). Russell also became a high steward of Oxford University in 1542 probably because university officials valued his friendship and the influence that he might exert at court. Joseph Foster, ed.,*Alumni Oxonienses* (rpt. Nendeln, 1968), III, 1291. Mrs. E.F. Russell has drawn my attention to the political overtones of the appointment.

3 See frontispiece. The Holbein drawing is in the Royal Collection at Windsor Castle. Two later portraits, one after the Holbein, are in the collection of the Duke of Bedford at Woburn Abbey and are reproduced in Roy Strong, *Tudor and Jacobean Portraits* (London, 1969), II, plates 41-43.

was to remain constant during the last years of the reign. The French were gathering forces ominously in Picardy, James V of Scotland refused to recognize the English succession, and unrest plagued the northern counties. In March 1541, under the renewed spectre of a French-Scottish alliance, the lord admiral was commissioned to levy 4,000 men and transport them to Calais. In April he went with the Earl of Southampton, then lord privy seal, to Calais and Guisnes to inspect English fortifications and keep Henry informed about French military movements.[1] By early summer, the king hit upon another plan of action; he would make a great progress to the northern part of the realm, shore up affection among his subjects there and perhaps meet with James at York. Russell, back in England, was among those Privy Councillors who accompanied Henry on his journey, but the meeting with the Scottish king did not materialize. Then, in December 1542, Russell participated in the legal proceedings against Queen Katherine Howard, Henry's fifth wife.[2] Yet even this crisis did not arrest the drift towards war. Henry had already expressed concern about his northern neighbour. Failure in marriage made the king, and hence his court, all the more interested in adventure abroad; martial exploits would replace marital woes.

Russell was not a direct participant in the Scottish war, which broke out in late summer of 1542. As lord admiral, he naturally dispatched and provisioned English ships, but he did not share in the fighting under the Duke of Norfolk, the commander of English troops in the North.[3] Norfolk was accompanied by the Earl of Southampton, the leader of the vanguard or forward part of the English army. When Southampton died in December, Russell filled the office at court made vacant by his death, that of lord privy seal, and Norfolk wanted him to replace Southampton in the North as well.[4] But the king did not follow Norfolk's suggestion. Instead he chose his brother-in-law, Edward Seymour, to assume the post.

Russell soon gained an impressive command elsewhere. The Spanish and the French had been at war with one another since the summer of

---

1  Harris Nicolas, ed., *Proceedings and Ordinances of the Privy Council of England* (London, 1837), VII, 165; *L.P.*, XVI, 793, 808, 813; Kaulek, *Correspondence politique,* 329-30.

2  In late October when Henry and his retinue returned south, Russell had hosted a session of the Privy Council in his home at Chenies; *L.P.,* XVI, 1287. Soon thereafter he was among those given a special commission for the trial of Culpepper and Dereham; *ibid,* 1395.

3  *Ibid.,* XVII, 753, 771, 776, 820, 846.

4  *Ibid.,* 944.

1542. The Spaniards, seeking allies, regarded Russell as one of their friends at the English court. As early as June, the Imperial ambassador Chapuys recommended that Russell together with Southampton, Bishop Gardiner, and Lord Chancellor Wriothesley be given pensions; with very small sums, Charles could win their support since these men were already favourably disposed towards the Imperial cause.[1] In August Chapuys singled out Russell as the person 'near the king who is best inclined to us and is besides a great friend of mine'.[2] In the end, however, outside events rather than councillors' sympathies pushed Henry to a Spanish alliance. France and Scotland were linked through royal marriage and, in early 1543 when Scottish affairs seemed momentarily manageable, Henry found the prospect of invading France attractive. Russell was one of eight commissioners who negotiated the terms of a secret military alliance concluded in February and directed against the French. A joint invasion was to occur before June 1544. The emperor would march through Champaigne, the English along the Somme, and both lead towards Paris. Henry and Charles envisaged a glorious, splendid enterprise.[3]

During the summer of 1543, Russell assisted Henry in supervising Edmund Bonner's mission to the emperor, but Russell's main contribution to the war effort came in military rather than diplomatic terms.[4] Henry's army, assembled in the spring of 1544, was divided into three sections. That segment under Norfolk's charge included 13,000 troops. A second group of 16,000 was placed under Suffolk's immediate command although Henry planned ultimately to lead these troops himself. Russell headed the vanguard, consisting of 13,000 men. The troops were to include foreign mercenaries as well as English soldiers.[5] Like all the councillors, Russell was responsible for mustering a certain number of horsemen and footmen. The king also expected him as lord warden of the stannaries to levy 200 miners from the west for the campaign.[6]

The English troops reached France as planned by June 1544. But Henry had already decided to depart from the strategy outlined in the treaty of alliance. Instead of the march along the Somme to Paris, two

---

1  *Ibid.*, Appendix B, 23. Cf. 22.

2  *Cal. S.P. Spain*, VI(ii), 37.

3  *L.P.*, XVIII(ii), 526. See Scarisbrick, *Henry VIII*, pp.440 ff.

4  For Bonner's mission, see Inner Temple Library, Petyt MS. 538, vol. 47, fols. 1-9.

5  *L.P.*, XIX(i), 273(5). This entry lists Russell as leader of the rearguard but contrast XX(i), 621(4).

6  *Ibid.*, XIX(i), 273(1), 275(2).

sieges were undertaken: one conducted by Norfolk and Russell against the town of Montreuil; the other, under Suffolk's leadership, against Boulogne. The king's ultimate objective, if he had one, was not clear even to his own commanders.[1] Henry himself arrived in July to supervise the Boulogne campaign and in September witnessed the city's fall. The English victory, however, was bittersweet at best. The Montreuil siege proved a sloppy and, in the end, unsuccessful affair. With Norfolk and Russell in logistic trouble, Henry reluctantly ordered their retreat to Boulogne. After Henry returned to England in early autumn, Norfolk and Suffolk retreated further, withdrawing from Boulogne to Calais, much to the king's anger. Meanwhile even the successful Boulogne campaign had its price. Not only was the siege strategy financially expensive, but it also gave Charles an excuse to desert Henry and come to terms with the French.[2]

Russell thoroughly disapproved of much that went on in the 1544 campaign, a tribute to his own good sense. And he spoke his mind, another indication of how secure he felt in his relationship with Henry. Although his criticism was not unique, it reveals a sense of realism that contrasts strongly with Henry's own approach to war and diplomacy. Russell's displeasure became evident as early as 20 June when he complained to the Privy Council about supplies.[3] An unusually strong letter followed on 1 July, addressed to the king himself. By now Russell's complaints covered a whole range of topics: the Flemish were not providing enough food for English troops; the siege of Montrueil would be of little benefit without the capture of Boulogne first; the siege of Montrueil could not succeed because English troops had not thoroughly isolated the city and sealed all its gates. Russell remembered Henry's earlier wars against France, no doubt recalling the Tournai episode and the Bourbon alliance, misadventures that had cost the king 'no small charge'. And as for the current campaign 'hit may be called a wyld war . . . we do here but wandre dispending your Majesties treasor after this sorte without any gayne . . .'. In the end the campaign would serve as 'a great encouragement to the ffrenche men to sett lytle by any army that shall pass over hereafter'.[4] Writing on the same day to Sir Anthony Browne, Russell repeated these concerns, which were

1  *Ibid,.* 758. Scarisbrick, *Henry VIII,* pp. 446-47; L.B. Smith, *Henry VIII. The Mask of Royalty* (Boston, 1971), pp. 203-4.

2  Hall, *Chronicle,* p. 806;*Annales,* ed. Edmund Howes (London, 1631), pp. 587 ff.; *L.P.,* XIX(ii), 142, 237, 302, 252-54, 383, R.B. Wernham, *Before the Armada. The Growth of English Foreign Policy 1485-1588* (London, 1966), p. 158.

3  *L.P.,* XIX(i), 746.

4  PRO S.P. 1/189, fol. 151; *L.P.,* XIX(i), 816.

obviously on his mind. He had seen the king make four different voyages to France without acquiring one additional foot of territory, enterprises which succeeded only in bringing dishonour to the English crown.[1]

Russell's critique of Henry's military policy was a blunt statement, but the old soldier was still too good a politician not to cover his tracks. He began his letter of 1 July by asking the king for 'lycence to speg my poore fantastie and opinion' and ended 'beseeching your Majestie to pardon me of this my bold and rude writyng . . .'. Anxious lest his letter appear outspoken, he reassured Henry: 'your excellent wysdome hathe pondered in theis thinges a thounsande tymes more than my wytts are hable to comprehende'.[2]

Russell showed similar impatience restrained by tact in disagreements with Norfolk during those troubled summer days. On 16 July, he complained to the king that supplies continued to enter Montreuil because the gates were not being properly manned. He clearly had no faith in Norfolk's siege strategy and accordingly asked Henry to send Sir Anthony Browne, Sir Thomas Seymour, or Richard Cromwell to observe and report on the situation. He further requested Henry to thank the Flemish governor de Rue for procuring food supplies for English troops despite Norfolk's dissatisfaction with de Rue's performance. Russell reasoned that de Rue had at least tried to help the English and would appreciate an expression of gratitude. Norfolk's angry reprimands had led de Rue to threaten to abandon the English entirely, a warning that worried Russell. Moreover, since he and Norfolk disagreed about how to handle de Rue, Russell asked Henry 'to be a gostly father in this matter'. If Henry did not keep Norfolk in the dark, 'it should engendre a greate pyke between him and me: whiche needeth not, for I have ben very playne with him alredy dyvers tymes'.[3]

The fall of Boulogne in mid-September did not radically improve England's military and diplomatic position. A few days later the emperor concluded peace with the French by the Treaty of Crépy. One of the emperor's men, acting as mediator between the French and the English, approached Norfolk, Suffolk, and Russell during October. By November, however, the possibility of peace negotiations between England and France had collapsed, and Russell was back at Westminster.[4]

---

1    PRO, S.P. 1/189, fol. 153; *L.P.,* XIX(i), 817.

2    PRO, S.P. 1/189, fols. 151-52.

3    PRO, S.P. 1/190, fols, 45-46; *L.P.,* XIX(i), 919 and cf. 920.

4    *Cal. S.P. Spain,* VII, 225; *L.P.,* XIX(ii) 354, 365, 367, 432, 560-61.

Responding to the threat of a French attack on English soil, Henry ordered three new armies in the south, each containing approximately 30,000 men, again under the command of Norfolk, Suffolk, and Russell.[1] As might be expected, Russell's special concern lay in the southwest and, since the fleet was gathering there, his attention focused on naval matters. Acting as lord lieutenant, he was commissioned to supervise coastal defences and recruit mariners and ships to serve the king. The anticipated French armada not only made an appearance but also briefly landed on the Isle of Wight. The invasion threat ended, however, with some skirmishes off Portsmouth in August.[2]

Now in England, Russell remained convinced of the folly of the war. His sojourn to the west only reinforced his sentiments. He had to work hard to persuade unwilling seamen to give up private profit and join the king's fleet. And while Russell diligently performed his responsibilities, he also nursed personal grievances, for his travels put a drain on his pocketbook. Hoping for peace, he thought the best chance for ending the war in late July lay in another attempt by the emperor at mediation.[3]

Russell was hardly alone among Henry's Council in taking issue with the king's military policy. Norfolk, like Russell while still in France, had deplored the difficulties in conducting the war. Somewhat earlier Edward Seymour had advised Henry against the burning of Edinburgh.[4] By the summer of 1545, a group at court headed by Sir William Paget urged peace upon the king. Norfolk's stance may be explained by his pro-French sympathies; Russell and the other peace advocates simply felt that the nation would gain no advantage in continuing the war.[5] Russell was unique only as one of Henry's first critics and in speaking so bluntly.

Henry's own attitude contrasted sharply with the pragmatism of his councillors. In diplomacy as in religion, the king was less modern than some of his own advisers. Their realism, their concern for national self-interest, and their anxiety about England's limited resources found no reflection in Henry's medieval pursuit of honour and glory. Some of the councillors were themselves aware of the dilemma. Stephen Gardiner, a member of the peace party, worried that a dishonourable

1   *L.P.,*  XX(i), 958, 1078, 1081(33).

2   *Ibid.,*  1159, 1254-55, 1278, 1282, 1307; XX(ii), 6, 63, 204, 225.

3   *Ibid.,*  XX(ii)., 242; XX(i), 1255.

4   *Ibid.,*  XIX(i), 319.

5   Smith, *Henry VIII,*  p. 215.

peace might affect Henry's mental state ('the repose of his mynde'). As long as Prince Edward remained a minor, 'the decaye of his Majesties person . . . shuld be more ruine to the realme thenne any warre could engendre'. Writing in this melancholy mood in November, Gardiner dared not advise Paget on the best course to follow.[1]

Henry's military policies tarnished the end of his own reign and darkened his legacy to Edward. The king squandered two-thirds of his monastic wealth before concluding peace with the French in the spring of 1546. The English then consented to the restoration of Boulogne by 1554 upon receipt of 2,000,000 crowns, an empty victory as France never complied with the terms.[2] Although Russell was a major participant in the war, he cannot be blamed for most of its mistakes and errors. He hardly distinguished himself on the field (but neither did Henry's other commanders in France), and he was wrong when, in June 1544, he advocated Boulogne as the war's prime military target. Yet his criticisms were perceptive; he quickly recognized the futility of the war and justifiably emphasized its cost. His letters give the impression of a reluctant participant in an adventure that Henry foolishly devised and Norfolk clumsily executed.

In addition to his military responsibilities, Russell served as keeper of the privy seal, an office he held from the time of his commission in December 1542 until his death in 1555.[3] Remarking upon Russell's death, the Spanish ambassador thought the privy seal one of the four most important offices in the kingdom and assumed that Russell had been one of the great figures of state, apparently following in the very footsteps of Cromwell.[4] In fact, despite its prestige, the privy seal had been in a state of decline even in Cromwell's day. Seals were simply losing importance as government grew more modern and came increasingly to rely on signed letters in the conduct of its daily affairs. Moreover, Cromwell's own administrative reforms made the functions of the privy seal more a matter of routine and strengthened the signet at its expense.[5] Cromwell of course presided over the two seals simultaneously. Subsequent keepers of the privy seal, lacking his genius and the force of his personality, never matched his authority.

1   Stephen Gardiner, *The Letters of Stephen Gardiner*, ed. James Arthur Muller (Cambridge, 1933), pp. 187-88.

2   *L.P.,* XXI(i), 1014.

3   *Ibid.,* XVII, 1251(7); Thomas Rymer, ed., *Foedera, Conventiones, Literae,* 2nd ed. (London, 1728), XV, 155-57; *Cal. Pat, Rolls, Mary,* I, 208.

4   *Cal. S.P. Spain,* XIII, 158.

5   Elton, *The Tudor Revolution,* pp. 15, 52; Chapter IV, esp. pp. 274-76 and pp. 293-98.

When Russell became keeper of the seal, it had thus already lost its initiating, focal role in administration. It continued to be vital for many of the courts, for letters of summons, for forced loans, for departments of state without their own seals — all tasks which could be confined to the hands of the four clerks who served under the keeper. Otherwise the duties associated with the lord privy seal remained minimal. Custom established him as *ex officio* president of the court of requests but, as in so many of Russell's judicial posts, the title was more imposing than the duties.[1] For Russell the office of lord privy seal was important first for its prestige and patronage, a further indication that Russell had become one of the king's senior, trusted servants. Second, the office brought with it, beyond sealing fees, a yearly salary of £365, a generous figure that nearly trebled the 200 marks he had received as lord admiral. When added to his other fees and his landed income, it made Russell one of the fourteen wealthiest peers of the realm by 1545.[2]

At court the lord privy seal moved on a troubled stage. No one of Cromwell's stature emerged to assume the role of chief minister, and consequently domestic politics were especially volatile. Despite occasional interventions, Russell generally remained peripheral to the factional machinations dividing the court.[3] By the final year of Henry's life, a shift of power brought young men — notably, Edward Seymour, John Dudley, and William Paget to new prominence. Dudley, in his mid-forties, was the eldest of the group. The men of Henry's own generation — Russell, Cranmer, St John and Browne — in their late fifties stood somewhat aside from the centre of power. Significantly they still retained the king's trust and confidence. Indeed Henry may have found solace in their company, a reminder that he was not alone in facing old age.[4] But observers correctly sensed that the younger men

1 *Ibid.,* pp. 298, 134, 139. See also David A. Knox, 'The Court of Requests in the Reign of Edward VI, 1547-53', unpublished dissertation, Cambridge University, 1974, pp. 260 ff. For the staff of the privy seal office, see Henry Maxwell-Lyte, *Historical Notes on the Use of the Great Seal of England* (London, 1926), p. 38; T.F. Tout, *Chapters in the Administrative History of Medieval England* (Manchester, 1930), V, 76, 79.

2 Cf. *L.P.,* XVI, 475(2); XVII, 1251(7); Hellen Miller, 'Subsidy Assessments of the Peerage in the Sixteenth Century', *Bulletin of the Institute of Historical Research* 28 (1955), 18-21. It is impossible to measure fees and gratuities which the admiralty and privy seal brought. The lord privy seal and his four clerks divided amongst them the fees (1s. to 6s.8d.) derived each time the seal was used. See Knox,'The Court of Request', pp. 267-69 and Maxwell-Lyte, *Historical Notes on the Great Seal,* p. 34.

3 In 1546 Russell helped to save a Protestant courtier, Sir George Blagge, from imprisonment. See above, p. 42, n.2.

4 See discussion in Smith, *Henry VIII,* pp. 230-31 and Beer, *Northumberland,* pp. 20ff. Travelling in September 1546, the King took with him Russell and Browne as well as Seymour, Dudley, and Paget. When Henry was ill in January 1547, Russell was one

would be the most influential figures in the next reign. Russell's relationship with his junior colleagues during the late Henrician period is thus worth attention. From Dudley and Paget he received respect and friendship.[1] But with Edward Seymour, Earl of Hertford, Russell experienced some trouble.

Russell had deliberately cultivated Seymour's friendship when the latter had become the king's brother-in-law in 1536. Like his colleagues at court, he had given the new Earl of Hertford gifts and favours, first some fowl, then, in a gesture of goodwill, the use of his cook. Russell had also been careful not to antagonize him in his land dispute with his stepfather, Lord Lisle, who was usually Russell's client. These tactics apparently worked. Russell was among the Earl of Hertford's house guests during the late 1530s and at the end of the decade the two men dined together as friends.[2]

Yet Hertford was not an easy man with whom to deal. His temper, pride, and arrogance often bothered his colleagues, and tension eventually developed between him and Russell. In 1538 after the death of Hertford's sister, Queen Jane, Russell risked his anger and intervened for Lisle in a second property dispute.[3] Although no real problem emerged over the issue, by March 1544 the two men found themselves on opposing sides over a land grant involving the Bishop of Sarum.[4] Far more serious, they openly, even bitterly, quarrelled that month over a piece of crown property which one of Hertford's servants, a man named Crouche, wanted to lease. Russell seems to have coveted the same land. For whatever reason, he opposed leasing to Crouche and wanted the matter settled through the mediation of his friend St John and Sir Richard Southwell, commissioners for the sale of the king's lands.[5] Russell blamed Hertford's influence when Crouche after some vacillation rejected the mediation. In retaliation, the lord privy seal refused to deliver a licence that the Earl required for trade in woollens.

of the four councillors commissioned to assent in the king's name to Norfolk's attainder, *L.P.*, XX(ii), 11 ff; Rymer, *Foedera*, XV,118.

1   See e.g., PRO, S.P. 1/205, fol 121 or *L.P.*, XX(ii), 242. At one point, Russell and Dudley had a misunderstanding about the purchase of some wine, but Dudley carefully minimized the affair. PRO, HCA 1/33, fol. 261.

2   See Michael L. Bush, 'The Rise to Power of Edward Seymour, Protector Somerset, 1500-1547', unpublished dissertation, Cambridge University, 1967, and 'The Lisle-Seymour Land Disputes', pp. 264-65. also Longleat. The Seymour Papers, XVIII, fol. 44 or HMC, *Bath MSS.*, ed. Marjorie Blatcher (London, 1968), IV, 341.

3   Bush, 'The Lisle-Seymour Land Disputes', p. 271.

4   Longleat, The Seymour Papers, IV, fol. 4 or HMC, *Bath MSS.*, IV,97. Cf. *L.P.*, XIX(i), 188, 230.

5   *L.P.*, XIX(i), 277(5).

Hertford, who at this time also met resistance from commissioners in negotiating a land exchange with the king,[1] was in no mood to compromise with Russell.

The dispute can be followed in the correspondence of John Berwick, Hertford's agent in London. Writing to Hertford on 6 March, Berwick referred to the lease for the first time. He had himself assured Russell that Hertford had urged mediation upon Crouche. Whereupon Russell replied that he expected as much, 'otherwise ye shoulde do hym muche wrong for he sayeth he hathe ben allways youre ffrende . . . more than ever ye had the knowledge of'.[2] Subsequent letters took no notice of the affair, but on 25 March Berwick raised a second issue, the licence that Hertford sought. The king had already signed it, the signet passed it, and the licence was now in the hands of the lord privy seal, who Berwick hoped would cause no delay.[3] On the morning of 27 March, however, Russell made technical excuses to explain why he could not deliver the licence. Significantly, when Berwick mentioned Crouche to him, Russell expressed resentment. He complained that Crouche had been willing to refer the dispute to mediation until he had spoken with Hertford. Even when Berwick suggested that Crouche be examined under oath, Russell was certain of Hertford's complicity. Moreover, Russell was further angered and offended over rumours that Hertford had threatened him. According to Berwick, Russell had learned from a third party 'that ye perceyved . . . he bore youe mallyce or grudge, and . . . yf yo put yn a fynger ye woulde put yn body and all . . .'. For his part, Russell felt he had been Hertford's friend, intervening on his behalf even with the king, speaking 'more yn youre causes than youre owne brother'. Berwick concluded that Hertford must himself write to Russell if the lord privy seal's anger were to be appeased.[4]

Unfortunately, Hertford's letter did more to deepen than to heal the quarrel. Its tone smouldered with such bitterness and self-righteousness that Paget advised Berwick against delivering it. But when the licence was further delayed, Berwick saw no alternative.[5] In the letter Hertford denied ever speaking the threatening words attributed to him. As for Crouche, if Russell were a real friend, he would take Hertford at his

1   Longleat, Seymour Papers, IV, fols. 41 ff.; the exhange dispute is treated by Arthur Slavin, 'The Fall of Lord Chancellor Wriothesley: A Study in the Politics of Conspiracy', *Albion*, 7 no. 4 (Winter 1975), pp. 270-71.

2   Longleat, Seymour Papers, IV, fol. 42; HMC, *Bath MSS.*, IV,91.

3   *Ibid.*, fol. 56 and p. 95.

4   *Ibid.*, fol. 60 and pp. 96-97.

5   *Ibid.*, fol. 68 and p. 101.

word. Hertford demanded to know Russell's decision about the licence 'for I entend to disguise with no man and had rather have an open enymy than a feyned frende'.[1] Not surprisingly, Russell found Hertford's tone arrogant, but after consulting with Paget, he delivered the licence on 9 April.[2] He then took the first step towards reconciliation by writing a letter which apparently soothed Hertford's temper. Russell's note does not survive, but Hertford's response on 21 April was friendly. He expressed his confidence in Russell, was satisfied with the licence, and declared himself ready to do Russell's pleasure.[3] Meanwhile, marking the end of the affair, Crouche found himself imprisoned on 17 April.[4]

Such disputes were common enough among an aristocracy immersed in land acquisitions and litigation. Yet the quarrel had additional importance, influencing Russell's opinion of Hertford and thereby contributing to the politics of the next reign. Hertford's manner and personality were generally more abrasive and offensive than Russell's. Although twenty-one years junior to the lord privy seal, in this incident Hertford had not refrained from provocative language, and he had insisted that Russell make the first gesture towards reconciliation.

A few years later, upon the death of Henry VIII, Russell and his colleagues at court accepted Hertford's appointment as lord protector. As the new king's eldest uncle and a proven, competent soldier, Hertford was a natural candidate for the position of protector. But Russell's support may well have been shrouded with tacit reservations. He could hardly have felt the same deference and loyalty for Hertford which he had formerly given to Henry VIII. The lord privy seal had seventeen years more experience at court than the lord protector. Aware of the importance of tact and goodwill in the art of government, Russell knew at firsthand how sharply and offensively Hertford could treat his peers. Moreover, Russell was dependent upon the protector for neither wealth nor title. As one of Henry's 'new men', Russell would never be committed in quite the same way to any other monarch, let alone a mere protector.

Henry's will of 30 December 1546 became his last testament and ensured Russell's participation in the opening of the new reign. Russell was named as one of sixteen executors all of whom were to sit on Edward's Council. He also received a legacy of £500, matching the

1 *Ibid.*, fol. 5 and pp. 97-98.
2 *Ibid.*, fol. 76 and pp. 101-2; *L.P.*, XIX(i), 442(7).
3 Longleat, Seymour Papers, IV, fols. 6-7; HMC, *Bath MSS.*, IV, 104.
4 *Ibid.*, fol. 82 and p. 103.

sum granted to Hertford, Dudley, St John, and Wriothesley. Cranmer received 500 marks whereas the ten remaining councillors, including Secretary Paget, got £300 apiece. Otherwise Henry treated the executors as equals, for he singled out none for a preeminent position in his son's reign.[1] Yet whatever the king's intentions, the will's provisions about a regency council were not even temporarily respected.

Henry died on 29 January 1547, but the councillors kept the news secret for three days. Finally on 31 January, Wriothesley announced Henry's death to the court and Paget read aloud parts of his will. Russell was among the councillors who proclaimed the death to the London populace.[2] Later that day, 31 January, the new Regency Council met and named the Earl of Hertford as the protector of the realm. Although the councillors stipulated that the lord protector 'shall not do any acte but with the advise and consent of the coexecutors', they also gave to Hertford the 'furst and chief place amonges us'. They argued that a protector would insure the safety of the king, provide orderly, efficient government, and conduct effective diplomacy. Hertford deserved the appointment because of his 'proximitie of bludde' with the king as well as 'the great experience which he hath in all affayres of this realm . . .'.[3]

Russell supported but did not initiate the critical political moves in the days after Henry's death. His signature was one of thirteen subsequently added to the Council's minute of 31 January, but his role in these machinations is impossible to discern. Hertford, uncle to the new monarch, and Paget, confidante of the old king, were the key allies in the scheming that took place. Upon Henry's death, the earl left London with Sir Anthony Browne to fetch Edward from Hertford. They then went to Enfield House where they remained until 31 January, during which time Edward learned of his father's death. In London Paget sought the support of Russell and the other executors, who remained ignorant of much of the intrigue. Hertford may have contemplated making some alterations in the contents of the will, which so far only he and Paget had seen. The rest of the Regency Council did know of Hertford's whereabouts and even corresponded

1 L.P., XXI(ii), 634. Cf. Lacey Baldwin Smith, 'The Last Will and Testament of Henry VIII', *Journal of British Studies* 2 (November 1962), 14-27; Mortimer Levine, 'The Last Will and Testament of Henry VIII', *The Historian* 26 (August 1964), 471-85; and Elton, *Reform and Reformation,* pp. 331-32.

2 Edward VI, *The Chronicle and Political Papers of Edward VI,* ed. W.K. Jordan (Ithaca, 1966), p. 4: *Cal. S.P. Spain,* IX, 6; BL, Harl. MS. 353, fol. 3.

3 *APC,* II, 5.

with him. By 31 January they were ready to support his appointment as protector and, the next day, earl and king returned triumphantly to London.[1] Only Wriothesley, the lord chancellor, initially hesitated to support Hertford, and even he accepted the minute of 31 January. Sir Thomas Seymour, brother of the protector, then demanded the governship of Edward. Hertford refused, wanting to keep control of Edward together with the office of protector. But as a compromise, he admitted Seymour to the Council on 2 February and thus amended Henry's will on questionable authority.[2]

The participants in these events soon found themselves the recipients of valuable honours. On 15 February, less than a week before Edward's coronation, eight councillors accepted new titles and estates. The Earl of Hertford became Duke of Somerset; Dudley, already Lord Lisle, was named Earl of Warwick; and the Earl of Essex, Wriothesley, Seymour, Rich, William Willoughby, and Edmund Sheffield were also elevated in rank.[3] Russell belonged to a second group of officials who, although given no peerages in February, nonetheless received separate land grants during the summer of 1547. Russell gained a reversionary grant to the manor of Woburn in Bedfordshire, lands worth £100 *per annum* which would become the chief family estate for future generations.[4]

Why did Russell receive no new title in February 1547? Although obviously political rewards, the grants allegedly reflected the wishes of the late king. According to Paget's testimony, Henry had wanted to acknowledge faithful servants and also replenish the depleted ranks of the nobility by redistributing the lands anticipated from the Duke of Norfolk's attainder. Henry's original list of prospective candidates stipulated Lord Russell and Lord St John, each to receive earldoms and lands worth £200. But like some other nominees, they were 'not well satisfied, some laboureng to remayne in their olde degrees, and others thinkeng the land to litle for their mayntenance . . .'. Henry had there-upon dropped their names and even entertained second thoughts about the project as a whole.[5] According to Paget, then, Edward's Council was

1 Edward VI, *Chronicle,* p. 4; PRO, S.P. 101/1, fols. 1 and 3. Russell's name does not figure prominently in contemporary sources. Van de Delft, for example, first mentions him on 7 March; *Cal. S.P. Spain,* IX, 49.

2 D.E. Hoak, *The King's Council in the Reign of Edward VI* (Cambridge, 1976), pp. 23-34. Hoak suggests that Dudley encouraged Seymour's action.

3 *APC.* II, 34-35.

4 *Cat. Pat. Rolls, Edw. VI,* I, 6-7. St John received a comparable grant; *ibid.,* pp. 42-43.

5 *APC,* II, 15-22.

left with the opportunity to act upon Henry's revised list of nominees. Yet, although Paget's testimony was probably true in its general outline,[1] Russell, St John, and the others surely waited until after Henry's death to refuse their titles. Well into February the Regency Council, or at least Hertford, continued to consider different options. A list dated 15 February, the very day that the honours were distributed, initially included Russell as Earl of Northampton with £200 in lands.[2]

Whether or not he initiated the revision, Russell willingly accepted Woburn in lieu of a greater title. Somerset granted Wriothesley an earldom and would not have risked antagonizing Russell over the matter; his support was too important. Perhaps Russell and his colleague St John acted magnanimously to avoid additional financial pressures on the crown.[3] Whatever his motivation, Russell was satisfied enough with the Woburn grant, itself no mean prize. The incident underlines his attitude towards the new reign: the lord privy seal remained very much his own man. Henry VIII had provided him with a great office of state, a position of eminence in the west, and comfortable wealth. His career could continue for the time being on its own momentum. He accepted the protectorate on grounds of political stability rather than reasons of simple self-interest. Relinquishment of the earldom in February like his unobtrusiveness in late January suggests that he was not a prime mover in Somerset's ascendancy.

England was to have a king who reigned and a protector who ruled. Edward's coronation took place on 20 February with Russell officiating as high steward.[4] But on 7 March the Imperial ambassador concluded that the protector 'governs everything absolutely'.[5] With Russell's acquiescence — and that of St John, Cranmer, Warwick, Browne, Sir William Herbert, and Sir Anthony Denny — Somerset had already deprived Wriothesley of the great seal.[6] A patent on 12 March enhanced and secured his authority. In addition to Somerset, six Councillors signed the Register on 13 March, recognizing the patent. Russell was among this group and one of those immediately readmitted to the new

1    On 23 January, while Henry still lived, the Spanish ambassador had mentioned rumours of new titles. Also lending credence to the testimony were Sir William Herbert and Sir Anthony Denny, two gentlemen of the privy chamber whom Paget cited as witnesses. *Cal. S.P. Spain*, IX, 4 and *APC*, II, 15.

2    PRO, S.P. 10/1, fol. 28.

3    Pollard, *England under Protector Somerset*, pp. 29-30.

4    *Cal. Pat. Rolls, Edw. VI*, I, 181.

5    *Cal. S.P. Spain*, IX, 48.

6    *APC*, II, 48-57.

Council.[1] The Regency Council had been transformed, indeed demoted, into an ordinary Privy Council, whose decisions were no longer binding, whose membership the protector might alter at his discretion. Moreover, as recent scholarship indicates, Somerset pursued a personal style of government, consulted Privy Councillors at his convenience on a random basis, and thereby weakened the Privy Council itself as an institution.[2] Russell's contribution must be understood within this general context. He served as a senior and respected member of the government but, as in Henry's reign, he did not make policy decisions.

In February 1547, predicting the chief men on the Council, van de Delft, the imperial ambassador, omitted Russell's name. But a year later, he wrote very differently, calling Russell 'very influential here and especially in the matter of [trade] claims, he being the oldest [sic] member of the council'.[3] Van de Delft correctly singled out Russell's age as a key to his prestige although, to be more precise, it was age coupled with experience. The lord privy seal was sixty-two years old in 1547 whereas the average age of the Privy Councillors was forty-seven. Some were older than Russell, namely Sir John Gage and Bishop Tunstall, but neither was as active as the lord privy seal. Moreover, although an experienced group, no one on the entire Council had served longer than Russell's forty-one years.[4]

His first sustained assignment enmeshed him in diplomatic negotiations and illustrates the nature of his contribution and service. Already contemplating war against Scotland, Somerset anxiously wanted to alleviate tensions with France. On 4 March Russell received a commission together with Warwick, Thomas Seymour, and Paget, to negotiate over fortifications in Boulogne and to discuss the possibility of a defensive league with the French. The sessions, sometimes held in Russell's house on the Strand, accomplished little of substance. A treaty of amity was ratified by 12 March, but the death of Francis I meant that it was not put into effect.[5] Russell was probably not unduly disappointed, for his own sentiments seem to have been pro-Imperial.[6] His inclinations,

---

1   *Cal. Pat. Rolls, Edw. VI,* I, 97; *APC,* II, 63-64; Hoak, *The King's Council,* p. 44.

2   See Hoak, *The King's Council,* esp. pp. 260, 267-68.

3   *Cal. S.P. Spain,* IX, 19 and 258.

4   Jordan, *Edward VI,* 1, 82-83. St John was the same age as Russell but had entered court in 1528; *DNB,* XV, 537-38.

5   *APC,* II, 47-48, *Cal. S.P. Spain,* IX, 49; Odet de Selve, *Correspondance politique de Odet de Selve, ambassadeur de France en Angleterre (1546-1549),* ed. Germain Lefevre-Pontalis (Paris, 1888), 128-36.

6   See above, p. 46 and p. 42, n,8.

however, did not affect English diplomacy. Although the English commissioners were theoretically of equal stature, Paget was the pre-eminent diplomat among the councillors during Somerset's tenure.[1] To him and the protector belonged the domain of foreign policy, and often he was involved in moves and strategies about which his colleagues knew nothing. Russell in contrast was conerned with the everyday operation of policy, not its creation.

Throughout Somerset's ascendancy, Russell remained a working member of the Council. In the summer of 1547, when Somerset left the court to command the English army in Scotland, he included Russell among five councillors with whom the French ambassador might confer in total confidence. Paget again took the leading role when Boulogne fortifications were discussed, but Russell regularly participated in the talks.[2] Other preoccupations, most notably Russell's concern with issues of trade, reflected interests derived from the Henrician period.[3]

Somerset's absence from court was marked by the growing importance of his brother, Sir Thomas Seymour, lord high admiral. The story of Seymour's rise and fall is a well-known episode in Edward's reign, a tale of arrogance, ambition, and retribution. Russell played a secondary but interesting role in the Seymour affair, one that casts some light on his own ambitions and motivations. During 1548 both men exchanged favours and dealt with each other in that informal, friendly fashion characteristic of court relations.[4] In fact, Russell had not hesitated to question the lord admiral and give him fatherly advice when rumours linked his name with Princess Elizabeth.[5] Yet, when the Council considered the various charges against Seymour in January 1549, Russell collected evidence and provided one of the several despositions which led eventually to an act of attainder and Seymour's execution for treason.[6]

1    *Cal. S.P. Spain,* IX, 48 and Samuel Rhea Gammon, *Statesman and Schemer, William, First Lord Paget-Tudor Minister* (London, 1973), 136-37, 142.

2    De Selve, *Correspondance,* 210-216. Sixteen councillors, including Russell, received a commission to govern the realm in Somerset's absence. *APC,* II, 115-18.

3    See PRO, S.P. 1/244, fol. 76; HCA 1/33, fols. 217-19; *L.P.,* XVI, 172, 188, 347; below, p. 124. Russell attended the House of Lords regularly and in November 1547 and 1548 served as a trier of Petitions. *Journal of the House of Lords* I, 293, 316, 321.

4    PRO, S.P. 10/4, fols. 87-88.

5    PRO, S.P. 10/6, fol. 44.

6    *APC,* II, 236-38; John MacLean, *The Life of Sir Thomas Seymour, Baron Seymour of Sudley . . .* (London, 1869), p. 75. Russell's deposition (PRO, S.P. 10/6, fols. 44-45 is printed in P.F. Tytler, *england under the Reigns of Edward VI and Mary . . .* (London, 1839), I, 145-46.

It would hardly be surprising if the lord privy seal had been some-what resentful of Seymour's climb to power. Even more than was customary, Thomas Seymour had risen at court through ties of kinship rather than merit and service. Russell may have been one of the new men, but his own slow progress still contrasted sharply with that of Seymour, twenty-three years his junior. Edward's younger uncle had become a gentleman of the privy chamber as late as 1537, more than ten years since Russell had first held the same post, some thirty years after Russell had first come to court. Yet by the summer of 1547, Seymour's influence was great enough to challenge that of the lord privy seal. In fact, during Somerset's absence Seymour served as lieutenant general of the south in preference to others like Russell with far more experience.[1] Russell's testimony in 1549 revealed that he and Seymour were conscious of their rivalry. Seymour had once put the issue bluntly: 'What will you say my Lord Privy Seal if I go above you shortly?' Perhaps Russell's reply was less honest: 'I ansered I wold be glad of his preferment and concernynge goynge above me I dyd not care so that he take nothinge from me'. He had been provoked enough at the time to report the conversation immediately to the lord chancellor.[2]

Russell resented not simply Seymour's preeminence but also his particular arrogance and high-handedness. Seymour's marital ambitions especially antagonized him, and here the lord privy seal was reacting against a type of hubris utterly absent in his own career. Again according to his own testimony in 1549, Russell had tried to persuade Seymour of the folly and danger inherent in his plans. In 1548 he had wisely advised, 'if ye go aboute any such thinge [as marriage with Elizabeth], ye take the means to undo your sealf . . .'. His own caution, his shrewdness, his sense of restraint, all were affronted by Seymour's scheme. Two different modes of action, two different types of ambition were at odds, a distinction that set Russell apart from both Seymours during the early years of Edward's reign.[3]

Russell's official activities and concerns were not confined to Westminster during Somerset's tenure. As political stability deteriorated under the protectorate, Russell had to face mounting problems in the west. The letters of Paget record the general problem; to his distress, religious uncertainty, dissatisfaction over economic policies, and pressures from war continually eroded the effectiveness of the govern-

1  *APC*, II, 117 and Pollard, *England under Protector Somerset*, p. 81; see also pp. 180 and 178.
2  PRO, S.P. 10/6, fol. 45; Tytler, *England under Edward VI and Mary*, I, 14546.
3  *Ibid.*, fol. 44 and I, 145.

ment. By March 1549, Paget's tone had become urgent: 'for Goddes sake, Sir, spare no man so the kinge may be well served . . .' . He suggested how authority might best be delegated and among his recommendations, the Earl of Warwick should travel to the north and Russell sent to the west, advice unheeded[1] The crisis came to a head in June 1549. Rebellion spread throughout the country, in part a reaction against the new Prayer Book, in part a response to socio-economic grievances. In late June, Russell left London with instructions to quiet the western shires[2]

Contemporaries recognized Russell's special position in the west and historians must do the same. His contribution to the Tudor state cannot be evaluated solely in terms of the court and council, for he also contributed to local government as it developed during the mid-sixteenth century. A decade had passed since he received the lands and offices associated with the Tavistock grant. The rebellions of 1549 present a logical moment to interrupt the narrative of his career as lord privy seal and consider his activities as magnate in the west. Not only did his concern with western affairs reach its climax during this period of unrest, but the year 1549 also marked a significant and permanent change in Russell's conduct and attitude towards the west.

1    William Paget, 'The Letters of William Paget of Beaudesert, 1547-63', ed. Barrett L. Beer and Sybil M. Jack, *CamdenMiscellany,* XXV Camden Society, Fourth Series, XIII (London, 1974), 27.

2    Pocock, *Troubles,* pp. 8-10.

# 4

## RUSSELL AND THE WEST

The crown's tenuous control over remote regions of the realm created a persistent problem in sixteenth-century England. As demonstrated in the Pilgrimage of Grace, feudal ties and social unrest presented greatest danger in the north, but the early Tudor monarchs worried about the west as well. For one thing, the western counties were especially vulnerable to possible foreign invasion. Secondly, the internal power structure in the west included a loyal but independent gentry and a commons far from passive. In such circumstances, royal control in the west might have disappeared entirely without solid aristocratic support. King Henry VIII depended upon his cousin, Henry Courtenay, Marquis of Exeter, to provide such support during the first three decades of his reign. Until Courtenay's execution for treason in 1538, his lands and offices ensured his position as the leading aristocrat, the role which Russell assumed in 1539.[1]

The king granted Russell a title, former monastic lands, and several western offices and then expected him to keep the western counties placated and obedient. Russell tried to comply. He remained the most eminent aristocratic figure in the west from 1539 until his death in 1555. During these sixteen years, his career in the western counties achieved varying degrees of success and passed through at least three distinct phases. For most of the first decade, official assignments occurred infrequently, usually when war threatened. Russell cultivated pleasant, informal contacts with the gentry and, except for times of military danger, left the west much to its own devices. Rebellion in 1549 disrupted this pattern and ushered in a second phase, as Russell struggled for nearly three months to suppress the Western Upring. The rebellion forced reassessment, for it revealed to Russell the limits of his own authority and the independence of the lower classes. His

---

[1] See Gladys Scott Thomson, *Lords Lieutenants in the Sixteenth Century: A Study in Tudor Local Administration* (London, 1923), pp.17-18; Joyce Youings, 'The Disposal of Monastic Property in Land in the County of Devon, with Special Reference to the Period 1538-1558', unpublished dissertation, University of London, 1950, pp.170, 4-7; Youings, *Devon Monastic Lands: Calendar of Particulars*, p. xxvi. Youings points out that the only peers with sizeable holdings in Devon, the Earl of Bath and the Marquis of Dorset, had their primary interests elsewhere. Devon, Cornwall, Somerset, and Dorset together comprised the Tudor West, but Devon was the most important of the counties.

career subsequently entered its third, final, and most effective stage. After 1549, he utilized the office of lord lieutenant in a new, creative way and appealed to several segments of western society, an achievement gone unnoticed by historians.

When judging Russell's results in the west, historians have rendered mixed verdicts, depending on their particular perspective and interests. Joyce Youings and Gladys Scott Thomson come to conclusions favourable to Russell's reputation. Youings, who sees the west as basically tranquil, claims that Henry simply chose the best man for the job; Russell satisfactorily filled the vacuum created by Courtenay's death.[1] Writing earlier, Gladys Scott Thomson remarks that after 1539 Russell's authority in the west was 'almost regal'.[2] Far different are the views of W. K. Jordan in his studies of the reign of Edward VI. Focusing on the crisis of 1549, the year of revolt, Jordan describes the Henrician design as a failure. Russell served as Privy Councillor and allowed his responsibilities in London to claim too much of his time. The western gentry, a small, relatively poor, independent group of men, did not provide an acceptable alternative for leadership. The Western Uprising itself reflected the continued existence of a power vacuum.[3] Like Youings and Thomson, Jordan does not consider Russell's contribution in the years after 1549.

Neither the enthusiasm of Youings and Thomson nor Jordan's negative verdict address Russell's entire career. To say that the Henrician design failed because of the events in 1549 is to pass judgement at mid-point. On the other hand, to call Russell's authority near-regal is to ignore the very real independence of both western gentry and commons. How shrewd a choice did Henry VIII make? Could a new figure still very much involved in court activities at the same time exert effective influence in the western counties? Russell's career evolved slowly, included both failure and success, and must be judged as a whole.

Before Russell was given the opportunity to act in the west, the responsibility had belonged to Henry Courtenay, a man with strong credentials for the job. Courtenay came from a family long prominent in the west. As participants in the Wars of the Roses, the Courtenays had watched their fortunes decline with those of the Lancastrians only to revive at the hands of Henry VII. Lord William Courtenay

1  Youings, 'The Disposal of Monastic Property,' p.278.
2  Thomson, *Two Centuries of Family History, p.163.*
3  Jordan, *Edward VI, I, 458.*

then married a Yorkist princess and subsequently fell from grace. His son Henry, however, born about 1496, enjoyed royal favour, succeeded to the earldom of Devonshire, and spent much of his childhood at court. The king welcomed him as Knight of the Garter in 1521, appointed him to the Privy Council in 1525, and named him Marquis of Exeter in 1528. Anxious to strengthen Courtenay's position in the west, the king also appointed him to the significant western offices: steward of the duchy of Cornwall, lord warden of the stannaries, keeper of Restormel Castle. In addition, Courtenay served as steward of other royal parks and manors and as constable of Windsor Castle. Although he owned lands in various shires, his holdings lay primarily in Devon and Cornwall.[1] By the time of his death, his possessions were worth some £3000 *per annum*.[2] But his very wealth, power, and proximity to the throne caused Courtenay's downfall. After allegedly corresponding with Cardinal Pole, he was executed for treason in December 1538.[3] His real crime lay in his blood – his mother, Princess Catherine, had been a daughter of Edward IV. Henry VIII, nervous after the Pilgrimage of Grace, felt insecure as long as his leading western aristocrat was also a potential rival for the throne.[4]

The execution itself caused hardly a murmur in the west; neither gentry nor commons expressed anger or threatened unrest.[5] But in 1539, when war with France seemed imminent, Henry found new reason to worry about the area. Courtenay's death had left a power vacuum in the west at the very time when a Catholic invasion seemed likely. Clearly the king had to find a magnate with sufficient importance and authority to promote stability.[6]

Rather than elevate a member of the resident gentry, Henry rewarded one of his servants at court whose loyalty he trusted. Russell

---

1   For a good account of Courtenay's background and career, see Rowse, *Tudor Cornwell*, pp.114, 234. For Courtenay's property, see *L.P.*, XIII(ii), 454, 754(2), 1001, 1002.

2   Miller, 'Subsidy Assessment of the Peerage in the Sixteenth Century', pp.18, 20; Helen Miller, 'Summaries of Theses. CCXII. The Early Tudor Peerage, 1485-1547', *Bulletin of the Institute of Historical Research* 24 no. 69 (May 1951), 90.

3   For Cromwell's evidence, see *L.P.*, XIII(ii), 954-62.

4   For an alternative view, see Elton, *Reform and Reformation,* p.280. Courtenay's execution not only relieved the king's anxieties but also increased his revenues. The crown assumed ownership of Courtenay's property and annexed several manors to the duchy of Cornwall. See Rowse, *Tudor Cornwall,* p. 80.

5   Rowse, *Tudor Cornwall,* p.239; Dodds, *The Pilgrimage of Grace,* II, 318.

6   Youings, 'The Disposal of Monastic Property', p.170 and *Devon Monastic Lands,* p. xxvi.

possessed several qualifications which made him attractive for the job. Unlike Courtenay, he enjoyed neither aristocratic birth nor an independent base of power. In addition to his reliability, he could claim some ties to the west in his family origins, his Dorset patrimony, his commission as sheriff for Dorset and Somerset in 1528.[1] By virtue of the grants of 1539, his stature rivalled Courtenay's former position in the west. The Tavistock lands increased his income to over £1200 *per annum.*[2] In July he was named steward of the duchy of Cornwall, warden of the stannaries, steward of Courtenay's lands in the crown's possession, and rider of Dartmoor Forest. In September more of Courtenay's former offices came his way when Henry appointed him keeper of Restmormel Castle, master of the deer hunts at Dartmoor and Exmoor, and keeper of several parks.[3] Moreover, the king gave Russell new forms of authority specifically devised in the spring of 1539: the lord presidency of the Council of the west and a commission to supervise coastal defences.[4]

Suddenly Russell had received significant new duties and responsibilities. The king's secretary, Thomas Cromwell, looked with special interest on the office of lord presidency. Cromwell established the Council of the West, over which the lord president presided, as part of a general scheme for local administrative bodies. He hoped that a resident council would promote tranquillity in the west. For Henry, however, the possibility of foreign invasion stood as a greater threat than rebellion. Consequently, the king was more interested in Russell's commission to supervise coastal defences than in his duties as lord president.[5] Russell's obligations, of course, embraced both spheres, and contemporaries could not always distinguish in which capacity he acted.[6] He would supposedly encourage stability, redress domestic grievances, and supervise coastal fortifications. in all thwart the potential rebel as well as the foreign enemy.

1 Thomson, *Two Centuries of Family History,* pp.143-46, 113, 148-56. Note that Princess Mary's Council, which was associated with the Marches of Wales, included a John Russell as its secretary, but this was a different man; see Thomas Pugh, *The Marcher Lordships of South Wales 1415-1536,* Board of Celtic *Studies,* History and Law Series, No. XX (Cardiff, 1963), p.296.

2 *L.P.,* XIV(i), 1354(13); PRO, E 315/418; see Youings, *Devon Monastic Lands,* pp.5-7.

3 *L.P.,* XIV(i), 1354(12) and XIV(ii), 264(17).

4 *Ibid.* XIV(i), 904(12), 398.

5 Joyce Youings, 'The Council of the West', *Transaction of the Royal Historical Society,* Fifth Series 10 (1960), 44-45, 48-49, 52, 55-56.

6 *L.P.,* XIV(i), 1331. Adding to the confusion, eleven of the twelve men who

The creation of the Council of the West implied a thorough and continuing role for Russell in the shires. The Council included eighteen members who were to meet regularly, acting in both a judicial and an administrative capacity to adjudicate complaints, make justice easily accessible to the poor, and enforce specified laws. The Council's authority extended to both civil and criminal cases and included the right to hand out standard punishments, such as the cutting off of ears. Its instructions were nearly identical to those for the Council of the North, reorganized by Cromwell after the Pilgrimage of Grace. Only Russell as lord president had the power to convene and direct meetings, to summon or excuse members. So important was the lord president that he deserved as much honour as the king '(kneeling only excepted)',[1]

The Council's first session met in September 1539 at Tavistock. Russell then spent the autumn travelling throughout the west and hearing about rapes, burglaries, and the like. He apparently took his responsibilities seriously, for he remained interested in some of these cases even after he returned to London.[2] By the spring, however, he had been appointed lord high admiral, and his new duties absorbed all his time and energy. By the summer of 1540, the Council of the West fell into oblivion quietly and painlessly. Although it was not formally abolished, it did not sit again. Given Cromwell's fall from power, a period of tranquillity in the west, and Russell's own reluctance to spend much time there, its demise was only natural.[3]

After the disappearance of the Council, Russell's official journeys into the west tended to coincide with military crises. He remained a prominent figure, for the insignificance of the Council as an institution did not diminish his personal influence in the region. The Council may have fallen into disuse, but Russell's lands did not.[4] His title of lord president now lacked substance, but he exerted authority through other offices and new commissions. And he could always deal directly

served with Russell on the commission to maintain coastal defences also sat with him on the Council of the West; cf. *L.P.*, XIV(i), 398 and 743.

1   For the instructions of the Council of the West, see BL, Cotton MSS., Titus, B. I, fols. 176-77; *L.P.*, XIV(i), 743. Cf. those for the North, *L.P.*, XIII(i), 1269. The best scholarly treatment is Youings, 'The Council of the West', pp.41-59.

2   *L.P.*, XIV(ii), 399; XV, 95, 180; Addenda I(ii), 1452.

3   Youings, 'The Council of the West', pp. 41-43, 56, 58. Cf. Caroline A.J. Skeel The Council of the West' *Transactions of the Royal Historical Society*, Fourth Series 4 (1921), 74-75, 79-80.

4   The point is made by both Youings, 'The Disposal of Monastic Property', p.279 and Skeel, 'The Council of the West', p.75.

with western residents: apart from any particular office and commission, Russell could exercise influence through informal contacts and connections, a standard technique in the Tudor mode of governing.

As early as 1539 the western gentry expressed fondness for their new magnate. John Rowe, one of the members of the Council of the West, described the countryside as 'well content' with its lord president. Writing to Cromwell when Russell entered the west in the spring, Rowe praised Russell's 'substantial wit, great experience, wisdom and gentle nature'.[1] His enthusiasm was shared by Sir Richard and Lady Grenville, the former claiming that the Courtenays were 'never more esteemed nor better beloved in these parties than his lordship is'.[2] Such reactions are understandable, for Russell cultivated congeniality as an important ingredient in his long and successful career. His contacts and good relations with western gentry continued in subsequent years. As already discussed, his circle of clients after 1539 included the Edgcumbes, the Trevanions, and the Pollards — all western families. Western residents sailed in ships he owned,[3] served as bailiffs and stewards on his estate, and were recipients of his patronage.

These connections were tested in June 1545, when Henry again sent Russell into the area, this time as lord lieutenant responsible for coastal defence and naval recruitment.[4] Henry was in fact experimenting with the lord lieutenancy, still a commission flexible in its jurisdiction. The king named three lieutenants at this time, Norfolk, Suffolk, and Russell, each charged with responsibility for a number of counties. Russell's commission cited not only Devon, Cornwall, Dorset, and Somerset but also Gloucester. Previous lords lieutenant had raised troops in a district or controlled troops already levied, but now in Russell's case for the first time, a lord lieutenant was charged with naval impressment.[5]

Although the country was at war and a French invasion feared, Russell found it difficult to convince reluctant seamen to abandon their own ventures to serve in the king's cause. He spent a frustrating summer, and by August he gladly returned to London.[6] Yet in the end,

1   L.P., XIV(i), 686. See Rowse, Tudor Cornwall, p.242.

2   L.P., XIV(ii), 105.

3   N.A. Wyndham, A Family History 1410-1688 (London, 1939), pp.61-62.

4   See L.P., XX(i), 1081(33); Rymer, Foedera, XV, 75.

5   Thomson, Lords Lieutenants, p.18.

6   See above, p. 49 and ibid., pp. 19-21.

he succeeded in gathering a respectable fleet at Portsmouth and, in the process, benefited from his contacts with the western gentry. He was on good terms with the sheriff of Dorset and Somerset, Sir John Horsey, who had also served on the Council of the West and who made the task of recruiting much easier.[1]   At least he could count on the cooperation of the gentry in establishing defensive bulwarks along the coast.

Russell relied most heavily on the gentry, but he did not ignore the townsmen during the late Henrician period. Exeter, especially, was the focus of much attention. Russell generally used Exeter as his head-quarters whenever he spent a fair amount of time in the west.[2] Recently made a county in its own right, the city was an important economic centre and the provincial capital of the west. Its wealthy mercantile elite managed to combine an intense civic pride together with a stead-fast loyalty to the crown. Although the city fathers had frequently argued with the Courtenays, their relations with Lord Russell remained most cordial.[3] Respecting the parliamentary independence of the city, he rarely interfered with corporation matters unless asked. The city fathers regarded him as their spokesman on the Privy Council. In 1539, he wrote to Cromwell and asked redress for certain Exeter merchants whose goods had been seized in Spain. He regarded the merchants as a reputable class whose needs deserved the attention of the Privy Council, and consequently his concern went beyond Exeter. The letter of 1539 also mentioned issues affecting traders in other western ports.[4] Petition-ing again in 1545, he asked that the merchants of Totnes be allowed to keep captured French goods.[5]

Cordiality and cooperation thus prevailed in Russell's relations with

---

1   Thomson, *Lords Lieutenants,* p.21. Russell had probably sold some property to Horsey; *L.P.,* XV, 282(1).

2   He would reside at what eventually became known as Bedford House, formerly the priory of the Dominican friars, although he also had a country home in the area. Youings, 'The Disposal of Monastic Property', pp.270-71. See below, p.209.

3   For the importance of sixteenth-century Exeter, see Wallace T. MacCaffrey, *Exeter, 1540-1640. The Growth of an English County Town* (Cambridge, Mass., 1958), esp. pp.8, 13-25, 162. For the Courtenays and Exeter, see *ibid.,* pp.2-5; Youings, 'The Disposal of Monastic Property', pp.21-22; Thomson, *Two Centuries of Family History,* p.189. Relations between Exeter residents and Russell were cordial.  See for example, Gladys Scott Thomson, 'Exeter and the Russell Earls of Bedford', *Devon and Cornwall Notes and Queries* 18 (Jan. 1932), 15; Youings, 'The Disposal of Monastic Property', p.280.

4   Bedford Office, Papers of the First Earl, 5A, fols. 31-32 (copy) and *L.P.,* XIV(ii), 190.

5   *L.P.,* XX(ii), 52.

both landowners and townsmen. Yet all the contacts so far described suffered from important limitations. After the demise of the Council of the West, Russell had few dealings with the commons. As lord warden of the stannaries, he mustered miners for an anticipated war with France in 1543.[1] At the siege of Montreuil in 1544, Russell's contingent of troops came from the western ports.[2] Inspecting western coastal defences in 1545, he asked Secretary Paget to provide overdue salaries for poor labourers at Weymouth and Poole.[3] Such occasional attention was, however, no substitute for the role originally envisaged for the lord president.

Here, in fact, was the chief drawback to Russell's entire relationship with the western provinces. During the decade 1539-49, his interventions, though effective, were sporadic, primarily confined to times of military crisis. Rebellion in 1549 taught the inadequacy of this approach. Russell had won the goodwill of western landowners and merchants but nothing else. The Western Uprising showed how little actual control lay at his disposal when the counties chose to act in an independent manner.

Soon after the death of Henry VIII in January 1547, the Regency Council tried to prevent further unrest in the west. As a precautionary move, the Council entrusted 'good order' to the Earl of Bath, Sir Thomas Denys, Sir Hugh Pollard, and Sir Hugh Paulet, all important western landowners.[4] The first overt trouble developed in April 1548, when Cornish residents of Helston attacked an unpopular archdeacon sent to enforce iconoclastic religious injunctions. But western gentry effectively stopped the disorder. Acting on behalf of the crown, Sir Richard Edgcumbe, one of Russell's friends, gathered men from the east, marched into Helston, and dispersed the large, threatening crowds. Other landowners, like Sir Richard Grenville and Sir Hugh Trevanion, also on good terms with Russell, received a special commission of oyer and terminer to try the rebels. Seven of the ringleaders were executed, and the west returned to calm.[5]

A year later, in the spring of 1549, Lord Protector Somerset heard

---

1   *Ibid.,* XVII(i), 579.

2   *APC,* I, 174-75. See also above, p. 46, n.6.

3   *L.P.,* XX(i), 1104.

4   Skeel, 'The Council of the West', pp.73-74. See also PRO, S.P. 10/4, no. 40; *Cal. S.P. Dom.,* I, 10.

5   PRO, S.P. 46/58, fol. 5; Anthony Fletcher, *Tudor Rebellions,* Seminar Studies in History, ed. Patrick Richardson (London, 1968), p.49; Frances Rose-Troup, *The Western Rebellion of 1549* (London, 1913), pp.70-84, 88.

ominous news about widespread riots that extended from York to Kent. His government correctly diagnosed most of these outbreaks as reactions against enclosures, disturbances inadvertently encouraged by Somerset's own anti-enclosure sentiments. Religion played an important part, however, in provoking the uprising in the west. On 6 June, an assembly of commoners became violent in Bodmin. The 'mob' grew, captured Plymouth, and marched into Devon where men were protesting against the Book of Common Prayer.[1] Although only moderately Protestant, the Prayer Book abolished the Latin service and thus represented a drastic change for the conservative west.

As rebellion spread through the realm, the government suddenly faced a crisis threatening its very existence. Not surprisingly, the lord protector turned to Russell, the lord privy seal, to suppress the revolt in the western counties. Russell received a set of instructions on 24 June and at about the same time was named lord lieutenant, a commission he had last held in 1545 to meet the threat of a French invasion. His new instructions now mentioned the danger of invasion as well as the need for 'good governance'. Speaking in generalities, the instructions offered little real guidance to meet the emergency on hand. Russell was told to consult with justices of the peace and other honest men in the west, to promote filial duty and respect there, and to enforce the Book of Common Prayer. Although given a commission of array, he should use persuasion and gentleness before raising troops. Later the government tried to promote order through price-fixing and enclosure commissions.[2]

Probably the government did not yet realize the extent of the danger in the west. Russell himself did not appreciate the seriousness of the revolt until he and a relatively small retinue of men reached the county of Somerset in late June. The lord lieutenant went first to Hinton St. George, the home of the Paulet family where he met with Sir Peter Carew, *en route* to London. Once apprised of the situation and the rebels' advance to Clyst St. Mary, Russell immediately wanted

---

1 Rose-Troup, *The Western Rebellion,* esp. pp.98, 104, 131, 139. Recent interpretations acknowledge the presence of socioe-conomic tensions as well as religious grievances in the west. See Fletcher, *Tudor Rebellions,* pp. 61-63.

2 Pocock, *Troubles,* pp.8-10, 17-18; *Cal. Pat. Rolls, Edw. VI,* II, 251. G.S. Thomson notes that the original commission has been lost and it is not clear from Russell's instructions what his exact title was. Thomson, *Lords Lieutenants,* p.26. Yet in correspondence between Russell and the Privy Council, he was subsequently addressed as the king's lieutenant in the west. See Pocock, *Troubles,* pp.40-46 ff. M.L. Bush suggests instructions were not naive but rather the policy of appeasement reflected military necessity and successful past experience; see Bush, *The Government Policy of Protector Somerset* (London, 1975), pp.84-89.

more troops and supplies.[1] Arguments soon developed between the lord lieutenant in the west and the Council in London. Russell lingered outside Honiton while on 2 July rebels began besieging Exeter; he delayed any engagement in hopes of gaining a larger army. On 10 July, the Council promised reinforcements, horsemen under the leadership of Lord Grey of Wilton as well as foreign mercenaries. Yet Grey was detained, involved in disturbances elsewhere. Upon the Council's urging, Russell did attempt to levy footmen from the west itself but with little success. The Privy Council, occupied with a series of simultaneous revolts, grew irritated with his requests and inaction. Finally, by late July, the Council claimed that reinforcements had increased Russell's force to nearly 4,000 men, about the same number as the rebel troops.[2]

The first serious confrontation erupted in Devon on 29 July at the Battle of Fenny Bridges, a few miles outside Honiton. The king's army prevailed. It was a hard-fought victory, costing the rebels at least 300 casualties. Had Russell persevered in the chase after the battle, the rebels could have been effectively routed, but he stopped the pursuit before reaching Exeter. Strengthened in early August by the arrival of Grey's men, his troops again achieved victory in a fierce and bloody encounter at Clyst Heath. The turning point came on 6 August; Russell's force relieved the city of Exeter from a six-week siege and thereby saved the city from starvation.[3] Yet even after this triumph, Russell allowed the rebels opportunity to escape to Samford Courtenay, making necessary further fighting not only in Devon but also in Cornwall and Somerset. The arrival of 1,000 Welshmen under Sir William Herbert on 17 August aided in the final battles, which lasted until 29 August.[4]

Despite the Council's orders to disband his forces, Russell kept them

---

1 Rose-Troup, *The Western Rebellion*, pp.158-59. Rose-Troup estimates that Russell's original force consisted of 800 men, but Rowse claims it was 'a few hundred at most'. Rowse, *Tudor Cornwall*, p.273.

2 Pocock, *Troubles*, pp.11, 16, 22-35, 40-45. For full military narative, see Julian Cornwall, *Revolt of the Peasantry 1549* (London, 1977). For troop numbers, see Cornwall, pp.135, 177-78; Rose-Troup, *The Western Rebellion*, pp.232-33, 236-37. Cornwall suggests a higher number for rebel forces than the Council's figures, perhaps 6,000; p.103. Relations between Russell and the Council are further discussed below, p. 84, n.3.

3 John Vowell, alias Hooker, *The Description of the Citie of Excester*, ed. W.J. Harte *et al.*, Publications of the Devon and Cornwall Record Society (Exeter, 1919), II, 84-90.

4 Jordan, *Edward VI*, I, 472-74; Rose-Troup, *The Western Rebellion*, pp.291, 296, 299-306; BL, Harl. MS.523, fols. 50-51.

intact as subsequently he supervised punishment of the rebels. The most prominent of the rebels were sent to London for execution whereas the vast majority of insurgents received a pardon[1]. But in between these two extremes, Russell oversaw the execution of a number of ringleaders to serve as examples to the west and deter future resistance. The punishments were brutally administered, at least according to the standards of a later age. Most notorious was the case of the vicar of St. Thomas, a rebel priest hanged in his own church tower while wearing his vestments. Even when Russell was not personally responsible for the deaths, as in Cornwall where his deputy Sir Anthony Kingston took charge of the proceedings, the lord lieutenant approved of the methods employed.[2]

Russell's effectiveness as a commander and military strategist during this period has been the subject of debate. He often employed delaying tactics and did not pursue the enemy quickly enough to prevent their regrouping. He under-valued the advice of a successful soldier like Somerset who suggested skirmishes, ambushes, cutting supply lines, and reliance upon horse rather than footmen[3]. Yet from his own point of view, Russell had difficult odds to overcome and 'lyved in more feare than he was feared'[4]. As early as 1536 during the Pilgrimage of Grace, he had shown extreme caution in proceeding in a hostile countryside. When this same caution re-emerged in similar circumstances in 1549, it no doubt limited his effectiveness as a soldier and commander. His talents lay in other spheres.

As the dangerous summer progressed, Russell speculated on conditions in the west that had allowed such unrest to spread. His attention turned to members of the gentry, men whose support he had been cultivating during the last decade. Had his approach been vindicated? The gentry certainly had behaved loyally, first in 1548,

---

1 Pocock, *Troubles*, pp.63-67; PRO, S.P. 10/8, fols. 85-86. Russell was to postpone a general pardon lest ringleaders go undetected, but he .could issue individual pardons.

2 See accounts of the slaughters in W.G. Hoskins, *Devon and its People* (Exeter, 1959), pp.83-84; Rowse, *Tudor Cornwall*, pp.282-86.

3 These criticisms are made by Jordan, *Edward VI*, I, 468-77 and Bush, *The Government Policy of Protector Somerset*, pp.92-93, 96. Cornwall's *Revolt of the Peasantry* is also generally critical. Sympathetic views include John Haywarde, *The Life and Reigne of Edward VI* (London, 1636), p.61; James Anthony Froude, *History of England from the Fall of Wolsey to the Death of Elizabeth* (New York, 1868-70), V, 170; Thomson, *Lords Lieutenants*, p.29; Rowse, *Tudor Cornwall*, p.273; Fletcher, *Tudor Rebellions*, p.53.

4 Vowell, alias Hooker, *The Description of Excester*, II, 82.

then during the most serious crisis of 1549. Only a few gentlemen had entered the ranks of the rebels.[1] Despite their support, however, their performance did not impress Russell. By this time he knew many of these men quite well. Grenville had been entertaining him as early as 1539; family names such as Pollard, Paulet, Denys, and Edgcumbe had appeared with his on the Council of the West. The lord lieutenant certainly appreciated their individual efforts as, for example, when Sir Peter Carew acted to quell the original revolt.[2] But he became disenchanted with the gentry as a group and felt that the landowners had failed to exert all the moral influence inherent in their social status. Russell blamed the natural leaders of society at least in part for the unnatural catastrophe of rebellion. Revolt resulted from the 'lack of good orders amongst suche as ought to rule the commons . . .'. Their failure in leadership contrasted strongly with the valour of the city fathers, who maintained morale and loyalty during the long siege of Exeter. Even with such bravery, the city had nearly fallen to the rebels, a crisis caused by 'the lacke of such aide and assistance as the gentlemen of the country should have given . . .'.[3]

Russell would thus have agreed that the rebellion in 1549 revealed a power vacuum in the west. In his own analysis Russell focused on the gentry, but it is just as valid to cite his own ineffectiveness and the failure of his own methods. The chain of authority from the Privy Council to the gentry to the commons was not working properly. Given Russell's sporadic contact with the gentry in the 1540s and his neglect of the commons, the breakdown is not surprising.

Nonetheless, excuses can be made on behalf of Henry's new noble. Russell had been associated with the west for a decade, perhaps not long enough to develop personal loyalties and foster royal authority on a firm basis. The causes of the revolt, involving religious and economic grievances, lay beyond the control of any one local magnate. Also, several other counties besides the western provinces experienced an unruly commons. Russell found fault with the gentry in the west 'as in other parts of the realm . . .'.[4] But the real power vacuum of 1549 originated in London itself, for the breakdown of law and order can be

---

1 *Ibid.*, 67. Ironically one of the few gentlemen traitors, John Berry, Esquire, had previously purchased lands from Lord Russell. See Daniel and Samuel Lysons, *Topographical and Historical Account of Devonshire* (London, 1822), II, 103.

2 Russell wanted Carew included among those chosen in August to serve as his adviser, but the request was not granted. Rowse, *Tudor Cornwall*, pp.274 280.

3 HMC, *Report on the Records of the City of Exeter* (London, 1916), p. 21.

4 *Ibid.*

traced directly to the policies of Somerset's government. The ultimate failure of leadership at the centre created the chaos in the counties.

Moreover, the troubles that surfaced in 1549 led to new patterns in Russell's relationship with the west which made his role there more crucial than ever. The events of that year provided an important education for him. Although disillusioned with the gentry, he gained renewed respect for the townsmen. Consequently, he began to show increased concern for Exeter and to act frequently on behalf of its inhabitants. The rebellion also taught him the danger of ignoring the lower classes and thereby sensitized him to their grievances. After 1549, he remained more involved with the commons, a rare practice since the demise of the Council of the West. He used the office of lord lieutenant to reflect many of these changes in policy and behaviour. Russell's association with the west must be seen from this larger perspective; 1549 was a turning, not a terminal, point.

Relations between Russell and the Exeter city fathers had always been cordial, but the Western Uprising cemented the connection[1]. The city had earned Russell's gratitude during the rebellion. When the siege was lifted in August, the lord lieutenant embraced the mayor and his brethren and commended their service to the crown[2]. Not only had the city fought valiantly, but also individual merchants had loaned Russell money and extended credit when funds from the central government were delayed[3]. In September, he wrote to London and praised their bravery in defending the city[4]. For all practical purposes, the rebellion had been broken once Exeter was secured. Thus the uprising revealed the city's loyalty and at the same time underlined its strategic importance. Both factors explained Russell's appreciation and solicitude during the months that followed.

The lord lieutenant in Devon and the Privy Council in London showered attention upon Exeter in the aftermath of the rebellion. Russell sent letters of advice to the mayor and corporation. Gentry were appointed to counsel the mayor and prevent a further outbreak of violence.[5] In 1550, the Privy Council rewarded the city for its loyalty and past services by granting it the manor of Exe Island, formerly a

---

1   MacCaffrey, *Exeter*, p.206.

2   Vowell, alias Hooker, *The Description of Excester*, II, 90.

3   MacCaffrey, *Exeter*, p.206; *APC*, II, 318. Three merchants were involved and, in addition, the Mayor lent Russell £1000, on behalf of the city.

4   HMC, *City of Exeter*, p. 21; MacCaffrey, *Exeter*, p.206.

5   HMC, *City of Exeter*, p.21.

Courtenay possession. All ancient charters, privileges, and liberties were also confirmed while the mayors, bailiffs, and commonalty of Exeter received formal incorporation.[1] John Hooker, the city's historian, later suggested that Russell's recommendations had brought the benefits.[2]

For the remainder of his life, Russell continued a cooperative, supporting policy. In January 1550, when he was about to leave England to negotiate with the French, Russell, who was now styled the Earl of Bedford, wrote to his 'very lovinge friends', the mayor and city fathers. He expressed again the government's gratitude as well as his own good will and asked that Exeter members of Parliament be in London upon his return in order to advance the city's interests.[3] In June he was once more corresponding with the mayor and encouraging the city to build a tilt-yard for sports.[4] When in 1551 the townsmen planned a canal, the lord privy seal, 'not a litell gladd', praised its progress.[5]

In his role as benevolent adviser, Russell did more than encourage and patronize the city. In one instance, during a land dispute, he reprimanded the corporation for its behaviour.[6] On occasion he became the recipient of favours from the city fathers. For example, in 1553 when Russell wanted the Prince of Piedmont 'gentelye entertained', he prevailed upon the mayor.[7] In 1554, the earl saved the city from a costly piece of hospitality. Escorting Prince Philip on his journey to England with a retinue of 600 men, Russell managed to arrange a landing at Southampton, perhaps for the convenience and safety of the prince but at the same time sparing Exeter much effort and expense.[8]

Not only did his involvement in Exeter's affairs assume a more regular pattern after 1549, but also his concern for the west in general markedly increased. He remained in Devon throughout September in

---

1  BL, Royal MSS. 18, Docquet Book, c.24, fol. 26 or HMC, *City of Exeter,* p.24; MacCaffrey, *Exeter,* p. 27.

2  Bodleian Library, Rawlinson MSS., c.722, fol. 13.

3  Royal Letters and Other Papers, Exeter City Muniments, Letter 27. Taken from the microfilm collection at the Widener Library, Harvard University, Reel 65, A-3; see also HMC, *City of Exeter,* p. 22 and MacCaffrey, *Exeter,* p. 207.

4  HMC, *City of Exeter,* p.24.

5  Exeter, City Muniments, Widener Library, Reel 65, A-3; HMC, *City of Exeter,* p.27.

6  *Ibid.,* p.34.

7  *Ibid.;* MacCaffrey, *Exeter,* p.207.

8  Thomson, "Exeter and the Russell Earls of Bedford," p. 15; see below, p. 98.

the wake of the rebellion and, as the violence diminished, his attention naturally turned from military to administrative duties. The Privy Council had appointed six local advisers in August to help him discharge his responsibilities. In addition to punishing rebels, his duties included redistributing their forfeited lands, giving recognition to deserving subjects, taxing reluctant ones, advocating redress of certain grievances, and enforcing the new Prayer Book. The Privy Council did not give the lord lieutenant a free hand in these matters. He was to consult only with the six advisers specified by the crown and not others. Lest he prove too magnanimous, Russell was informed that he had no authority to adjudicate upon local suits and petitions. Moreover, the Privy Council often upbraided him or overrode his actions.[1]

Limitations to his power should not, however, obscure a significant development. The old Council of the West, while never revived, now began to cast a long shadow.[2] Russell showed a new sensitivity to the needs and frustrations of the rural poor, a group that he had virtually ignored since the demise of the Council of the West. The lord lieutenant in the west assumed judicial and administrative functions reminiscent of the former lord president. Russell showed interest in the grievances of the commons because he wanted to avoid a repetition of the violence of 1549. He was thinking less of the general social welfare than the promotion of social tranquillity. Yet Cromwell had established the Council in 1539 precisely on these grounds, to ensure tranquillity in the western shires. In several respects then, after the Western Uprising, the office of lord lieutenant took on new dimensions, in part overlapping with the old lord presidency.

In the weeks after the rebellion, Lord Russell advocated repeal of the sheep tax. It is easy to dismiss his actions as an example of pure self-interest. Repeal would have helped the established landowner and farmer, not the very poor, and would have worked to Russell's own

---

1 Rose-Troup, *The Western Rebellion,* p.294; Pocock, *Troubles,* pp.49, 52-56, 63, 68-70.

2 David Pill does claim that the Council of the West was revived, but he speaks casually and offers no evidence; Pill, 'The Diocese of Exeter under Bishop Veysey', M.A. thesis, University of Exeter, 1964, p.313. Caroline Skell notes that the Council was an important precedent that exerted influence in 1549 although Russell was then holding a military, not a political, office; Skeel, 'The Council of the West', p.80. This interpretation is nearer the mark. Professor S.T. Bindoff has been kind enough to show me the transcript of a letter written by Sir Gawen Carew on 10 August 1549 in which a council is mentioned; Thynne Papers, II, fol. 121. But I believe the letter refers only to the advisers helping Russell in the aftermath of the uprising. I find no evidence that the Council of the West as such was recreated.

economic advantage.[1] But the very poor were on his mind. Consider his letter of 30 September 1549, written from Exeter and addressed to Sir William Godolphin, Sir Hugh Trevanion, and other members of the gentry who served as justices. Russell claimed that he had heard 'sondry grevonces and horryble commplayntes' from the county of Cornwall. The poor were being impoverished by their landlords 'and the hole comyns universally vested with . . . oppressyon . . .'. What the lord lieutenant demanded seems strikingly modern: 'justice and equite (withoute respect of persons) shall appertayne'.[2]

Impressive parallels exist between the sentiments expressed in the letter of 30 September and Russell's former responsibilities as lord president. The Council of the West had been created to make inexpensive justice available to the poor. According to the instructions of 1539, the lord president should be ready to hear the case of 'the poorest men against the greatest lorde . . .'. The Council was 'to take such order that the pore people be not oppressed'. It was not to be a passive body which merely waited to receive complaints. Instead, members were to take the initiative, protect the interests of the commons, consider the problem of enclosures, and make enquiries into illegal renting.[3] Here, too, in the important matter of initiative, parallels existed between 1539 and 1549. In his letter of 1549, citing the authority of his current commission, Russell ordered the western justices to consult together not only to redress injuries already committed but also to prevent future wrongs.[4]

Hereafter Russell especially exploited his commission as lord lieutenant to wield influence in the west country. Although he used the lord lieutenancy in a new way, the position itself was not new. It evolved in typical English fashion during successive reigns in response

1 The issue is a confusing one. Originally devised as a progressive tax to control enclosure, in practice it hurt the smaller farmer, not the rich. See Fletcher, *Tudor Rebellions*, p.62. For Russell's position, see Pocock, *Troubles*, p.67. On 25 September, the Council agreed that only those with 100 sheep should pay the tax; Pocock, p.75. The tax was totally repealed in the next Parliament, perhaps due to Russell's influence; Rose-Troup, *The Western Rebellion*, pp.359-60.

2 Part of this letter is transcribed in Thomson, *Two Centuries of Family History*, pp.199-200. I am indebted to Mrs. M.P.G. Draper, archivist at the Bedford Office in London, for finding the original; Bedford Office, Papers of the First Earl, 5. The letter was also signed by Sir William Herbert and Sir Hugh Paulet, two of the six advisers appointed by the Privy Council to assist Russell (see Pocock, *Troubles*, p.52). Nevertheless, Russell was the main author. He uses the first person and refers to the commission he received form the king, presumably the lord lieutenancy.

3 BL, Cotton MSS., Titus, B. I, fols 176-77; *L.P.*, XIV(i), 743.

4 Thomson, *Two Centuries of Family History*, pp.199-200.

to the needs of the time or the demands of a certain region.[1] Consequently, the scope of the office escapes precise definition. Originally a military appointment, it included administrative responsibilities in Henry's reign. Russell's own commission in 1545 illustrates how flexible the office could be. His main tasks were naval recruitment and defence but, in addition, he became concerned with disturbances in Dorset and supervised the activities of JPs there.[2] In general, the commission came to serve a dual purpose, to guard the countryside from the threat of internal rebellion and to protect it against invasion.[3]

During Edward's reign, particularly during the period of Northumberland's ascendancy, the lord lieutenancy came into its own. After 1550, Northumberland attempted to make the office a permanent feature of local administration throughout the country. Northumberland had risen to supremacy within the Privy Council in the wake of the great unrest and resistance and, for this reason, he made a practice of sending experienced Privy Councillors into their home counties as lords lieutenant.[4] While Northumberland's prime concern was the suppression of sedition, Russell used his commission broadly to strengthen his position in the west.

Unlike his first decade as western magnate, Russell travelled to the west on official business frequently and regularly after 1549. He was sent there in April 1550 to guard against disorder. The Privy Council Register referred to him at this time as lord president, but he served in the capacity of lord lieutenant.[5] In the following February, the Council decided to discharge unneeded forces stationed at coastal fortresses. It divided this work according to regions and selected the lord admiral, the lord warden for the Cinque Ports, and the lord privy seal to work on the project. Once again Russell supervised the western provinces.[6] When in April 1551 the government grew uneasy, fearing

---

1 Thomson, *Lords Lieutenants,* pp.1, 111. For a discussion of the military origins of the office, see pp.11-13. The history of the lord lieutenancy paralleled the earlier development of the JPs. For the relationship between the two officiees, see Alan Harding, *A Social History of English Law* (Baltimore, 1966), pp.68-73.

2 *L.P.,* XX(ii), 159, 186, 190; Thomson, *Lords Lieutenants,* p.19.

3 See Russell's instructions of 1549 in Pocock, *Troubles,* p.8.

4 Thomson, *Lords Lieutenants,* pp.35, 30-31; W.K. Jordan, *Edward VI,* vol. II, *The Threshold of Power* (Cambridge, Mass., 1970), 57-61; *Cal. S.P. Spain,* X, 108.

5 *APC,* III, 6 or PRO, P.C. 2/4, fol. 5. Sir William Herbert had just been named lord president for Wales, and this fact probably explains reference to Russell's former office.

6 *APC,* III, 225.

renewed disturbances, it appointed nearly thirty lords lieutenant and instructed them to investigate treasons, oppressions, riots, felonies, 'and other evil dedes'. The commission was re-issued in 1552 and 1553, each time including Russell.[1]

Dispatched to the west to promote domestic stability, Russell had ample opportunity to enhance the authority of the lord lieutenancy. Early in the Henrician regime, Russell had served as a link between the western provinces and the government in London. Now it was as though in his person he brought the Privy Council to the west. When John Veysey, Bishop of Exeter, resigned, for example, he did so 'by word of mouth, as it seems, to the Earl of Bedford, being lord lieutenant of those western counties'.[2]

Russell's letter of 30 September 1549 implies that judicial matters claimed an important part of his attention. Other evidence survives which shows him playing the role of judge. A land dispute developed in August 1550 between two brothers, Jeffrey and John Buse. Jeffrey, the plaintiff, issued a bill of complaint to Russell as lord privy seal and lord lieutenant. Ultimately, after hearing the arguments of both parties, Russell declared in favour of the defendant. The very pettiness of the case is significant. It reveals that the lord lieutenant did more than suppress seditious activity. Jeffrey Buse described himself in his bill of complaint as 'a verie poore man and not hable to sew in the law . . .'.[3] Russell was thus resurrecting the obligations and responsibilities given earlier to the Council of the West: providing cheap, accessible justice for the poor. Once again he expanded the commission of lord lieutenant to include authority formerly delegated to the lord president.

Of course Russell did not always act solely in his capacity as lord lieutenant. As lord privy seal, he nominally headed the court of requests and, although rarely exercising judicial initiative there, he did intervene in a few cases concerning residents from the west.[4] Other

1 BL, Royal MSS. 18, Docquet Book, c.24, fols. 89-90, 208; also *APC*, III, 258-59; IV, 49, 276. In 1552 Russell also served as lord lieutenant for Buckinghamshire where he owned considerable property.

2 John Strype, *Ecclesiastical Memorials*, II(i), 424; see *Cal. Pat. Rolls, Edw. VI*, IV, 36. Just as significant perhaps was the fact that Veysey was succeeded by Coverdale who had accompanied Russell as chaplain during the Western Uprising.

3 DRO, W 1258, G 1/13, fol. 1. This document includes the proceedings of the case; it is a copy, probably by a seventeenth-century hand.

4 PRO, Req. 2/14/3, item 11; Req. 2/14/176. In another instance, Russell intervened because the plaintiff was one of his servants; Req. 2/14/103, item 3. Cf. Knox, 'The Court of Requests in the Reign of Edward VI', pp.78-79.

such incidents suggest increased involvement with the commons. In September 1551, the lord privy seal intervened to gain the release of two men in Exeter accused of spreading seditious rumours.[1] When King Edward made the only progress of his reign in the summer of 1552, he travelled as far west as Dorset, perhaps encouraged by Russell, who accompanied the king on his journey.[2] In Dorset the Privy Council heard a bill of complaint from a widow allegedly deprived of her property rights, and the lord privy seal attempted unsuccessfully to redress the grievance.[3]

Russell had still other offices through which he could legitimately wield influence in the west. As lord warden of the stannaries, he had jurisdiction over the system of special courts used by the tin miners in Devon and Cornwall. Usually wardens delegated this authority to others and, except for cases of judicial appeal, had few dealings with the miners themselves. But here, too, the events of 1549 indicate a turning point. The miners were among the poorest and most wretched members of western society, and they suffered severely from the effects of inflation. Under such circumstances, many of them had participated in the Western Uprising.[4] Their resistance in 1549 made an impression on the government. Acting to deter future unrest, the Privy Council issued a directive to Russell to gather together before him, or his deputy, twenty-four of the wealthiest mine-owners 'to refourme all such lawes and customes as be amisse . . .'. Unfortunately, the outcome of the project is not known. But the Council meant business, for it repeated its directive in a letter sent the following June.[5]

Once Mary became queen, Russell's appearances in the west grew

---

1 *APC*, III, 356. Also during this period, Russell acted upon a request of Tavistock residents and obtained licences for two annual fairs there whose profits might fund a school-master. DRO, W 1258, GE 1/8; *Cal. Pat. Rolls, Edw. VI*, 162; Finberg, *Tavistock Abbey*, pp.274-75. A proviso to a clothing act of 1552 exempted Tavistock clothiers from statutory regulations and guaranteed brisk trade at those fairs. Bedford sat on the parliamentary committee created after the first reading of the bill and was no doubt responsible for the Tavistock proviso. *Journal of the House of Lords*, I, 420; 5 Edward VI, c. 6 (XXIX).

2 *APC*, IV, 98-118.

3 PRO, Req. 2/15/69. Early in Mary's reign, Russell wrote to the Exeter city fathers on behalf of one Martin Barbaunce, who, he felt, had wrongfully been dispossessed of his land. See above, p. 75, n.6.

4 Rowse, *Tudor Cornwall*, p.62.

5 BL, Royal MSS. 18, Docquet Book, c. 24, fols. 24 and 111. See also Strype, *Ecclesiastical Memorials*, II(i), 485-86.

rare. His absence can be explained on several grounds. First, the queen made less use of the commission of lord lieutenant than had Northumberland. Second, Russell helped to arrange Mary's marriage and travelled abroad in 1554. Finally, in January 1555, he became seriously ill. He died that March at the age of seventy. Yet during his last years he maintained his western ties. His correspondence with Exeter inhabitants was as frequent as ever. In his role as lord warden, he dealt with supplications from the miners.[1] No doubt he was pleased that the west now remained tranquil. Despite Peter Carew's plans, Wyatt's rebellion met no successful response in the western shires.

In summary, it can be said that Russell's relationship with the west was complex, falling into at least three stages: his abortive lord presidency and occasional interventions during the 1540s; his suppression of rebellion in 1549; and his growing involvement in western affairs after the uprising. While historians have treated the first two stages, the third has been neglected. After 1549, the commission of lord lieutenant was expanded and used as a device for exerting judicial as well as military and administrative authority. Some of the purpose, if not the substance, of the Council of the West was resurrected. The commons began to receive a greater share of attention. New appreciation was given the city of Exeter, and the Privy Council talked of reforming the stannaries.

Many of these activities may have been born out of paranoia or insecurity on the part of Northumberland's government, but the results in the west country were positive. Although Russell did not initiate all these changes, he did take full advantage of them. Local government in Tudor England was not rigid, and Russell had opportunity to evolve his own approach. Working in a fluid context, he played his role both conscientiously and flexibly. He showed himself able to adopt new methods and assume new duties as the situation demanded. By mid-century, John Russell, first Earl of Bedford, was acting in a way that would have pleased his former royal patron.

[1]  *APC*, IV, 422.

# 5

## THE FINAL YEARS

The last half dozen years of Russell's life coincided with a period of extreme political and religious uncertainty within England. His performance was what one would expect from a shrewd, faithful Henrician: diligent service and ultimate loyalty to the dynasty in return for handsome rewards and political survival. His control of the western army gave him a large degree of influence in the *coup* of October 1549, which brought down the Duke of Somerset, but he did not initiate the process of political change. Thereafter as the Earl of Warwick consolidated his power and then later as Mary came to the throne, Russell's particular achievement was first to win an earldom, then to survive the change of regime. Yet his work for the crown had its own importance. Service performed by Russell and colleagues on the Council lent stability in the midst of religious, political changes.

Circumstances gave Russell the opportunity to play a decisive role in the *coup* of 1549. No sooner had the various rebellions of the summer been suppressed than the lord protector faced another challenge to his authority, this time a rebellion of sorts within the Privy Council. Only Cranmer, Paget, and Sir Thomas Smith sided with the protector, and even their loyalty did not last long. First at Hampton Court, then at Windsor, Somerset withstood the open opposition of the lords in London for only a week: by 14 October he was in the Tower.[1] After some initial vacillation, Russell and his companion in the west, Sir William Herbert, used the troops at their disposal to seal the protector's fate.

The Privy Councillors nursed a variety of complaints against Somerset. Many at court discerned in his behaviour an arrogant tendency to act as though he were king. His hesitancy to share favours and patronage with his colleagues aggravated their dislike. More significantly, they blamed Somerset's policies for the near collapse of government by 1549. War against Scotland had created fiscal burdens and imposed severe restraints on his administration. Somerset's concept of social justice — his opposition to enclosure and his association with

---

[1] *Cal. S.P. Spain*, IX, 457. For a contemporary narrative, see A.J.A. Malkiewicz, 'An Eye-Witness's Account of the *Coup d'Etat* of October 1549', *English Historical Review* 70 (October 1955), 600-9.

the commonwealth group – the councillors mistook for a threat to the hierarchic society, and the revolts of 1549 confirmed their innermost fears of social disturbances.[1] Nor did the protector's religious policy win him friends. The Prayer Book of 1549 was meant to be moderately Protestant and as comprehensive as possible. Unfortunately, radical Reformers as well as religious conservatives remained dissatisfied with the settlement. The Earl of Southampton, the Earl of Arundel, Sir Richard Southwell, and Sir Thomas Arundell joined the *coup* in hopes that it would lead to a more conservative church, a mistake on their part.[2] From a coalition of these different interests and grievances, opposition against Somerset solidified.

The conspiracy began in September, but only gradually did Somerset realize his precarious position. Not until 5 October did he respond publicly. Acting in the king's name, he issued a warrant to Sir Henry Seymour to raise troops and bring them to Hampton Court. Yet Somerset was not anxious to depend upon an unruly mob for his defence. He preferred to rely upon the troops already assembled in the west and firmly in the control of Russell and Herbert, whom he requested to advance to protect the king.[3] On the next day the protector, his nephew, and their small entourage withdrew to Windsor, where supplies and provisions were scarce.[4] No doubt at Somerset's behest, Edward himself now appealed to Russell and Herbert 'to macke withe all spede for our defence in this our necessitye . . .'. Edward promised to receive their help 'most thanckefully'. Somerset added to this letter a personal plea assuring Russell a future reward would he but 'shew the parte of a trew gentleman and of a verie frende . . .'.[5]

It is unlikely that Russell had joined the plot against the protector by 5 October. True, he had refused to obey Somerset's orders in mid-September to disband his troops, but the last sparks of the Western Rebellion had lasted into September, reason enough for Russell to retain the men under his command.[6] After all, he was a careful military strategist, often to the despair of his colleagues.

---

1 BL, Add. MSS. 48126, fol. 3. See discussion in Bush, *The Government Policy of Protector Somerset*, pp. 73-83.

2 *Cal. S.P. Spain*, IX, 458; X, 7. John Ponet, 'A Shorte Treatise of Politike Power', (1556), p. 133 in Winthrop Hudson, *John Ponet. Advocate of Limited Monarchy* (Chicago, 1942).

3 Pocock, *Troubles,* p.77-78.

4 Malkiewicz, 'An Eye-Witness's Account', p.607.

5 Pocock, *Troubles,* pp.79-80, 83.

6 Contrast Jordan, *Edward VI*, I, 516.

Moreover, upon receiving Somerset's letter of 5 October, he seems to have genuinely feared for the king's safety. He and Herbert initially complied with Somerset's pleas. By 7 October they had advanced as far as Andover, forty miles from Windsor. Only at this point did they seemingly reverse themselves, denying aid to Somerset in a letter of 8 October.[1]

After the crisis ended, Russell received handsome compensation for delivering his support to the Earl of Warwick, the ultimate victor in the political intrigues of 1549-50. Like other participants in the *coup*, Russell was generously reimbursed for recent expenses on behalf of the crown. In mid-January, he was named Earl of Bedford and given as a free gift lands worth £300 *per annum*. Six months later, in June 1550, the Privy Council cancelled a debt of £1,300 that he owed to the crown.[2] All told, Russell received much greater gifts and favours during Warwick's ascendancy than he had enjoyed during the protectorate. Nevertheless, financial considerations alone do not explain his motivation in October 1549. The protector had rather openly promised rewards in his letter of 6 October'.

Russell's response to personalities was probably at least as influential as the prospect of financial rewards in determining his decision that October. The dispute of 1544 may have lain dead and buried, but events during the Western Uprising revived some of the old rancour between Russell and Somerset. Tensions accumulated throughout the summer months, for Somerset and the Council in London tended to see the Western Rebellion in terms far different than did Russell down in Devon. The two parties argued on a host of issues: military tactics, reinforcements, supplies, and prisoners. Both Somerset and Russell could justifiably feel themselves harried and misunderstood. The protector had to contend with several simultaneous revolts as well as war with France. From Somerset's point of view, Russell's demands often appeared short-sighted and selfish. On his part, Russell felt that he had been sent into the west with unrealistic instructions, inadequate supplies, and too few troops. Once there, he seemed ignored or offered patronizing advice; funds were delayed.[3] Even after military

---

1  *Ibid.;* PRO, S.P. 10/9, fols. 47-49; Pocock, *Troubles*, p.91.

2  Gammon, *Statesman and Schemer*, p.167; *Cal. Pat. Rolls, Edw. VI*, III, 162, 43 and PRO, E 318/24/1415; *APC*, III, 52.   Russell also received episcopal lands in January 1550; see below, p. 112.

3  On 27 July, the Council in London responded harshly to Russell's request for ammunition: 'ye must understand that the more arrows ye use except good heade be taken the more ye furnysh your ennymie...'. The Council, led by Somerset, also disagreed with Russell about the deployment of horsemen: 'how wise and

hostilities ceased, the disputes did not subside. When Russell refused to execute one of the rebels, a brother to Sir William Paget, Somerset angrily observed that he had not spared his own brother for a similar offence.[1] When Russell redistributed lands confiscated from rebel leaders to reward loyal followers, the Council reprimanded him.[2] Russell would have been less than human had these personal grievances and irritants not influenced his stand a few weeks later in October.

Russell and Herbert explained their position in their own terms in a letter to Somerset on 8 October. Once reassured by the lords in London 'that no hurte nor dyspleasure is meant towards the kings majestie', they saw no reason to act on Somerset's behalf. They now realized that his argument with the councillors 'procedeth only upon pryvate causes . . .'. The only alternative to a *coup* was the unacceptable one of prolonged civil war. Like their contemporaries, they saw internal strife as a 'plage . . . sent unto this realme from god . . .'. Hence, given the safety of the king and the security of the realm, they would not lend troops to perpetuate the conflict.

> Wold god all maynes were used rather than any bludd shedde; which yf be attempted, And the case brought to that misery that the handes of the nobelitie be once poluted eache wythe others bludde, the quarrell once beganne will never have ende tyll the realm be dyssended to theat woful Calamytie that all our posteryte shall lament the chaunce.[3]

Russell's attitude in October 1549 was thus based upon a variety of factors not very different from those motivating the other councillors. Personal considerations, matters of policy, basic principles — all exerted an influence and together made his decision logical and natural under the circumstances.

When Somerset learned of Russell's reversal, he recognized the

valyant a capteyne a man is, yett to here the Counsiall of another can do no hurte. And we think us to have some experience in these things'. On the very next day, the Council notified Russell that Herbert would be arriving with one thousand footmen. 'The which request semeth straung'. In mid-August after the siege of Exeter had ended, Russell refused to reduce the western army. The Council argued that the army consumed too many supplies and would be more useful elsewhere. On 24 August they complained that if Russell "knewe as moche as we do herein presently see (and yet ye can well gess yt)", then he would surely yield on these points of contention. Pocock, *Troubles*, pp.41, 40, 44, 56. See also pp.47, 54-55, and 63.

1  *Ibid.*, p.54.

2  Vowell, alias Hooker, *The Description of Excester*, ii, 91; Pocock, *Troubles*, pp.68-70; Rose-Troup, *The Western Rebellion*, p.372.

3  Inner Temple Library, Petyt MS. 536, vol. 46, fol. 467 and Pocock, *Troubles*, p.91.

hopelessness of his situation. The Council in London had not only written to Russell and Herbert but had also appealed to the mayor and aldermen of London and the county justices and sheriffs. On 8 October, the Council issued a public proclamation which chronicled Somerset's offences and crimes, culminating in that of treason.[1] Meanwhile, the lords in London were in touch with the court at Windsor; Sir Philip Hoby served as intermediary and delivered letters to Cranmer and Paget. In this situation, lacking the support of the western army, Somerset's only chance for retaining power lay with the commons, an alliance not palatable to him. Thus, on 11 October, he submitted to arrest, offering no resistance once his personal safety had been assured. On 14 October, he and five of his most faithful followers were committed to the Tower.[2] The *coup* had succeeded. Now that the danger of civil war was passed, Russell hoped to heal the breach afflicting the Council. In a letter of 11 October, after Somerset's surrender, he and Herbert offered to mediate, 'to do what maie be in th'uttermose of our poweres to worke some honorable reconsillacion ...'.[3] Their proposal could have given little comfort to the former protector.

Somerset's fall left unresolved the question of who would govern in his stead. By January the Earl of Warwick emerged as the dominant figure and remained the power behind the throne until the death of Edward VI in July 1553. He assumed the title Duke of Northumberland in 1551 but acquired no other great honours or offices to display his influence. The protectorship remained too fresh and too unpleasant a memory for Warwick to resurrect it. He took only the office of the president of the Privy Council, through which he was able to control the convening and procedure of the Council. Otherwise he ruled through faction, appointing supporters to the Council, removing potential enemies, securing strategic posts for friends within the privy chamber. Through such methods, Warwick influenced the king and dominated the Council, which in turn carried out the functions of government.[4]

Russell proved one of the councillors who provided Warwick with critical support, for the earl achieved his success only by defeating the intrigues of the religious conservatives in late autumn of 1549.

1 See *ibid.*, p.92, 95-101. Russell's signature appears on the document of 8 October although he was not in London; see Pollard, *England under Protector Somerset*, pp.250-51, n.1.

2 *APC*, II, 340-43; Malkiewicz, 'An Eye Witness's Account', pp.607-9.

3 Inner Temple Library, Petyt MS. 536, vol. 46, fol. 470 and Pocock, *Troubles*, pp.111-12.

4 *Cal. S.P. Spain*, X, 7, 20-21; Hoak, *The King's Council*, pp.97, 262-63.

Although he had earlier encouraged the conservatives as allies, Warwick now correctly saw them as a threat: they were plotting a Marian regency, a development that would have thwarted his personal and political ambitions. Emperor Charles V's refusal to support English claims to Boulogne made their policy still less attractive. Responding to the danger of a Marian regency, Warwick managed in November to have admitted to the Council, Thomas Goodrich, Bishop of Ely and Henry Grey, Marquis of Dorset, men of reformed religious views. Reconciled with Paget, he sought other friends on the Council. St John especially played an important role, perhaps showing his friend Russell how to react and also warning Warwick in December not to press for Somerset's execution; Southampton would use a trial against Somerset as the means to bring down Warwick as well.[1] Instead Warwick bided his time and then acted from strength. By 14 January, the first of the conservatives, the Earl of Arundel, was placed under house arrest. Van der Delft concluded that Warwick had acted with the explicit support of St John, Russell, and Rich.[2] On 19 January Warwick dispensed earldoms to both St John and Russell for support they had given since October. Two days later Bedford departed to France on diplomatic business. There he heard of the fall and confinement of Southampton, Arundell, and Southwell; Warwick had secured his own ascendancy. Somerset's readmission to the Council in early spring marked the end of the crisis, the denouement of the *coup*.[3]

Later Russell assumed a similar role, compliant but passive in the proceedings which culminated in January 1552 in Somerset's execution and Paget's fall from the Council. Although Somerset's trial was rigged, his intrigues against Northumberland were no fabrication.[4] Russell successfully steered clear of the rivalry between the two men and was not involved when Warwick decided to strike at his rival. In fact, Bedford was one of those councillors who had to be summoned to court in September and October of 1551 once Warwick's strategy had crystallized. As a peer, he passed judgement on Somerset, but his position at the trial remains unclear.[5] If as is likely, he followed the

---

1 Hoak, *The King's Council*, p.241-55. Hoak has unravelled this story for the first time. Southampton hoped to implicate Warwick in Somerset's confessed 'crimes'.

2 *Cal. S.P. Spain*, X, 8.

3 *Cal. Pat. Rolls. Edw. VI*, III, 162 and 4; *Cal. S.P. Spain*, X, 21, 72. St John became Earl of Wiltshire.

4 Somerset planned to strike at Northumberland through Parliament; Hoak, *The King's Council*, pp.73-76.

5 Jordan, *Edward VI*, II, 82-83; *APC*, III, 374-78; Bl., Royal MSS. 18, Docquet

path of least resistance and simply accepted the political realities against Somerset, he helped convict a man who at least threatened the precarious stability then achieved.

During Warwick's ascendancy, Bedford immersed himself in the work of the Council. Three areas — diplomacy, trade, and administrative measures — consumed much of his time and give a fair indication of the scope of his responsibilities. His diplomatic service continued in the same direction established during the protectorate. He left England on 21 January 1550, sharing a commission with Paget, Sir John Mason, and Sir William Petre; their mission, to secure peace with France, a peace which Warwick needed badly. Their instructions outlined England's general objectives: Boulogne might be ceded provided that English fortifications there be destroyed, the French pay their pension in full (2,000,000 crowns), two English forts in Scotland be preserved, and the marriage treaty between Edward VI and Mary, Queen of Scots, be duly recognized. The commissioners might exercise discretion in arranging the time and place for the delivery of Boulogne. Neither specific nor binding, the instructions envisaged various compromise settlements. Nevertheless, when the negotiations began, the commissioners were careful to keep the Council in London well informed and to seek its approval.[1]

Paget had correctly diagnosed the two protagonists as early as August 1549: whereas the French and their king were 'some what refreshed . . . we are exhausted and worne to the bones . . .'.[2] The English government, indeed weakened and harassed by internal unrest, was intent upon peace. Since France enjoyed the stronger position, from the start it prevailed in the negotiations. Paget took the leading role just as he had in the negotiations of 1547, but even his skill could not help the English cause. With the Privy Council's acquiescence, the commissioners settled for far less than their original goals: the French received Boulogne but promised in return to pay only 400,000 crowns. Still, the English gained peace with both France and Scotland. Speaking

---

Book, c.24, fol. 158. Somerset was originally accused of treason but convicted only of a felony. The charge of treason was dismissed at the trial since Somerset allegedly plotted against Northumberland rather than the king. The Duke of Suffolk argued against the treason charge. Other peers, not identified, argued that Northumberland, the Marquis of Northampton, and the Earl of Pembroke should not pass judgement as they were the very men against whom Somerset allegedly conspired. Haywarde, *The Life and Rayne of Edward VI*, pp.134-37; BL, Harl. MS. 2194, fol. 20.

[1]   BL, Cotton MSS., Calig., E, IV, fol. 275; Add. MSS. 4149, fols. 26-28; Paget, 'Letters', *Camden Miscellany*, XXV, 81-98.

[2]   Paget, 'Letters', p.77; cf. p.94.

for his colleagues, Paget concluded 'we have . . . taken what we may . . . contenting our selfs till God send better . . .'.[1] He and Bedford attended to some official business at Calais and were back in London by the end of March.[2]

In the case of Anglo-Imperial relations, diplomacy often embraced commerce, an area of interest and expertise for Bedford since the late Henrician period. He took part in negotiations when disputes developed between Flanders and England about piracy, tolls, and the authority of the Inquisition. In February 1548, during the protectorate, he and Paget had protested to Van der Delft about the seizure of English goods and seamen. Van der Delft did not refrain from 'a sharp passage or two' but secretly advised the emperor to yield the point, for English claims were legitimate and English trade essential to the citizens of Antwerp.[3] Nevertheless, friction continued and was aggravated after 1550 by the financial collapse of the Antwerp market. In January 1552, the Privy Council protested against the taxation of English merchants in Flanders. Because Spain was then at war against France, the Council could afford to be outspoken. The Duke of Northumberland threatened the Imperial ambassador, then Jehan Scheyfve, with the suspension of English trade to Flanders. Bedford reinforced Northumberland. Recalling that once the English had received far different treatment, he stated that if the Spanish persisted in current practices, they 'might as well take a stick and drive them [the English] out'. Bedford assured the ambassador that England would always 'find some corner to trade', foreshadowing the creation of the Muscovy Company in 1553 in which he was to be a shareholder. Indeed the fact that his own ships engaged in trade may have motivated his anger. Mincing no words, the lord privy seal claimed that the Flemish had more need of England than the English had need of Flanders.[4]

In addition to such international concerns, Bedford was also involved in domestic, administrative matters, for his work as a Privy Councillor remained diverse and unspecialized.[5] Recent scholarship suggests that despite its factionalism and opportunism, Northumber-

---

1  *Ibid.*, p.98. Treaty is printed in Rymer, *Foedera*, XV, 211-17.

2  *APC*, II, 373; BL, Harl. MS. 284, fol. 75 or Paget, 'Letters', p.97.

3  *Cal. S.P. Spain*, IX, 338-39.

4  *Ibid.*, X, 440. For the Muscovy Company and Russell's mercantile interests, see below, p. 124.

5  For example, Russell was one of the six nobles charged with attending the young king 'for the honorable education of his Highness in thies his tender yeres in learning and vertue . . . '. (*APC*, II, 344). In April 1550, he met and accompanied

land's government had to its credit a number of positive achievements. The traditional picture of an unscrupulous duke with an inefficient Council is being revised, and Northumberland instead emerges as a serious leader who dominated a docile but proficient Council. Critical to the re-evaluation is the importance attached to Northumberland's programme of rationalizing royal finances. In an attempt to restore the rapidly deteriorating financial position of the crown, Northumberland strove through a series of royal commissions to raise cash, survey the condition of the revenue courts, and embark upon a serious programme of retrenchment.[1] Bedford's responsibilities came to reflect these concerns.

First in January, then again in July and December 1552, Bedford and several colleagues received commissions to recover debts due to the crown in the various revenue courts. To expedite the recovery of the money, the crown initially ordered commissioners to question officials of the courts and examine court records. But when evidence was compiled and debtors examined, the results were unsatisfying. Thus in July commissioners were instructed not only to investigate debtors but also to punish those who refused payment and, if necessary, to seize their property. The king thought it only 'reasonable' that the debtors make good their obligations 'and not as they do, suffer themselves to grow further in debt'.[2] By the fiscal year's end, the procedure netted £16,667 in delinquent payments.[3] Bedford moreover served on commissions to survey and collect church bells, plate, and ornament, other means of raising revenue.[4] All told, the crown issued twenty-four commissions concerned with finance during Northumberland's ascendancy, including a major investigation of the entire revenue system in March 1552.[5]

Bedford was also named to legal commissions during this period. In

French hostages at Dover. [John Gough Nichols, ed., *Literary Remains of King Edward VI* (London, 1857), II, 259-60, note 1]. During the summer, he interrogated Bishop Gardiner and gave testimony against him. (Edward VI. *Chronicle*, p. 34; Foxe, *Acts and Monuments*, VI, 95, 98, 161-62, 180-82). In December he was commissioned to collect subsidies for Bedfordshire, Buckinghamshire, and London. *Cal. Pat. Rolls, Edw, VI*, V, 351, 360).

1   Hoak, *The King's Council*, pp.203-8, 266-68.

2   *Cal. Pat. Rolls, Edw. VI*, 356 and also 64, 144, 392; BL. Royal MSS. 18, Docquet Book, c. 24, fols. 179, 280-81.

3   Edward VI, *Chronicle*, pp.102-3, note 201.

4   *Cal. Pat. Rolls, Edw. VI*, V, 413-15; BL Royal MSS. 18, Docquet Book, c. 24, fol. 281.

5   See discussion in W.C. Richardson, ed., *The Report of the Royal Commission of 1552*, Archives of British History and Culture, III (Morgantown, 1974),

March 1552 with nine other special commissioners, he was empowered to oversee execution of the penal law, 'to consider which of the said laws are most necessary and to cause inquisition to be made for all sorts of offenders . . .'. The commissioners, or at least six of them, were instructed to assemble regularly and see that law officers adequately performed their duties. The government not only desired laws enforced for their own sake but also had in mind the revenues that would accrue from such enforcement[1] When, a few weeks later, the crown appointed another commission of ten, again Bedford's name appeared. Noting the burden of work afflicting the Council because of the great number of private suits and petitions received, the crown delegated authority to the special commissioners 'for the hearing, examining, and ordering of all suits' before they reached the Council proper. The task was less judicial than administrative, deciding which suits should be directed to the Council and which should be sent to other courts.[2]

As in other times, so during this period, Bedford was more conscientious than he was imaginative in carrying out assignments. His official position explains his participation in many of these projects. As lord privy seal and therefore *ex officio* head of the court of requests, he was a logical appointee to hear private suits and petitions. As an experienced councillor, he had developed administrative skills useful in the commissions which investigated revenue courts. Nevertheless, despite such involvement, Bedford promoted no fiscal or administrative innovations nor was he among those interested in reform of Council procedure.

· Bedford's attitude towards Northumberland's regime coloured his responses to the accession crisis of 1553. On the surface, everything in Bedford's relationship with Northumberland during these years was correct. No personal incidents reminiscent of the Somerset era engendered ill feelings, and judiciously distributed gifts kept the earl satisfied. Yet although he personally profited from the regime, Bedford showed no signs of genuine affection or enthusiasm for the duke. In January 1550, the Imperial ambassador, Van der Delft, accused him of opportunism, a charge more appropriate now than at any other period of his career[3] Bedford's actions in 1553 reveal how

pp.xxiii ff.

1  *Cal. Pat. Rolls, Edw, VI,* IV, 352-53; Hoak, *The King's Council,* p.203.

2  *Cal. Pat. Rolls, Edw, VI,* IV, 353. Little evidence survives of the work of the commission, which consisted of Privy Councillors and masters of requests; Knox, 'The Court of Requests in the Reign of Edward VI', pp.228-29.

3  *Cal. S.P. Spain,* X, 8.

weak was his commitment to Northumberland's cause, especially in comparison to his loyalty to the Tudor dynasty. Although Northumberland's government had achieved peace, maintained order, and initiated fiscal reform, it nevertheless smacked of greed and exploitation and, most telling, promised England no hope of lasting stability in the face of a disputed succession.

When Northumberland attempted legal changes that would have enhanced his authority and made his influence permanent, Bedford opposed him. Northumberland (then the Earl of Warwick) sought reform of the Council in January 1551. His scheme, whose details are not known, failed when it met resistance from Paget, Rich, Wiltshire, and Bedford, all of whom later became good Marians. Warwick wrote to Paget and agreed to drop the matter. He regretted that his plans were not materializing 'as well for the surety of the King's majesty as for the truth of the matter . . .'. At least the matter had been debated 'which I reckon even a happy thing . . .'. Warwick explicitly asked Paget to communicate his decision to the lord privy seal, an implication that Bedford's stance had been important to the outcome of the deliberations.[1]

Whatever the issue of contention in 1551, Northumberland's significant move came later in his attempt to amend the will of Edward VI. The king was seriously ill by the spring of 1553. Either on Edward's instigation or, more probably, that of the duke, a 'Device', drawn up in June, altered the succession to deprive Princess Mary of the crown. The Device bestowed the succession instead on Northumberland's daughter-in-law, Lady Jane Grey of the Suffolk line, and her male heirs. Northumberland had further strengthened his position through a series of political marriages that spring. Sisters of Lady Jane were betrothed to the sons of Lord Grey and the Earl of Pembroke; a Dudley daughter was promised to a son of the Earl of Huntingdon. Meanwhile Privy Councillors like Bedford received new gifts of land.[2]

Despite such precautions, Northumberland's plans miscarried. When Edward died on 6 July, success seemed assured. Jane was declared queen on 10 July. The duke had garrisoned troops at Windsor Castle and had already appointed the usual lords lieutenant. Mary, however, withdrew to Kenninghall in Norfolk when informed of her

---

1  Pocock, *Troubles*, pp.134-35; see Jordan, *Edward VI*, II, 51.

2  Inner Temple Library, Petyt MS, 538, vol. 47, fol. 316; Hayward, *The Life and Rayne of Edward VI*, pp.172-73. See below, p. 113, n.5.

brother's death and there claimed the throne in her own right. Several loyal supporters, such as the Earl of Sussex and Sir Edward Hastings, joined her as she proceeded to Suffolk. Northumberland, trusting no one else, took command of the royal forces. On 14 July he left London to meet Mary's troops, a fatal mistake. The councillors were beginning to vacillate, and their support for Northumberland did not survive his absence.[1]

On 13 July, seven councillors, including the lord privy seal, consulted secretly with the Imperial ambassador. The counter-revolution had started. Yet the Council was a cautious group that hesitated to act rashly. As late as 17 July, they were admonishing the sheriffs of Kent to stand firm behind Queen Jane; Lord Rich received similar exhortations on 19 July. Nevertheless, that very morning Rich informed the Council that the Earl of Oxford had joined Mary's camp. This news, coupled with gentry support for Mary, persuaded the rest. Shrewsbury, Arundel, Winchester, Bedford, Cheyney, Paget, Petre, and Mason withdrew from the Tower where they had been meeting and reassembled at the home of the Earl of Pembroke. Conferring there with the lord mayor and other London citizens they pledged their allegiance to Mary.[2] Bedford's personal stance during all these events is significant, first, because it typified the position adopted by other Henricians like St John (now the Marquis of Winchester), Paget, and Herbert (now Earl of Pembroke); second, because the episode casts a great deal of light on Bedford himself, his motives and his loyalties.

Although Bedford seems to have accepted Mary Tudor out of desperation only when her cause was on the verge of triumph, this impression needs qualification. Bedford never allowed abstract principles or ideology to dictate his political position, but neither did he in this instance act at the last moment and then out of sheer self-interest. He absented himself from Parliament and Privy Council meetings during the spring of 1553, a highly unusual move for him, perhaps because he already suspected Northumberland's plot and wished to avoid it.[3] Although he later signed the Device, the

1  Pollard, *The History of England from the Accession of Edward VI,,* pp.88-89; C. Sturge, The Life and Times of John Dudley, Duke of Northumberland, 1504-1553', unpublished dissertation, University of London, 1927, pp. 238-42.

2  *Cal. S.P. Spain,* XI, 88, 106; HMC, *Report of the Ms. of George Allan Finch, Esq. of Burley on the Hill Rutland* (London, 1912), 1-2; Strype, *Memorials of Thomas Cranmer,* II, 913; Charles Wriothesley, *A Chronicle of England during the Reign of the Tudors,* ed. W.D. Hamilton, Camden Society, XX (London, 1877), II, 87-89.

3  History of Parliament Trust.  Bedford was absent from the Council and the

evidence strongly suggests that he did so reluctantly, with resistance. On 24 June, three days after the signing, one of the Imperial ambassadors, Jehan Scheyfve, observed that Northumberland's plot would face opposition from certain councillors, and he singled out Bedford as one of these. On 4 July, only two days before Edward's death, Schyfve informed the emperor that the councillors had accepted the altered will out of fear. 'Lord Shrewsbury, the Lord Warden, the Privy Seal and other members of the government demurred and made many difficulties before consenting . . .'. On 19 July as the Council was about to declare for Mary, the Imperial ambassadors again observed that several councillors — Bedford, Pembroke, Shrewsbury, Arundel, Mason, Paget, and others — had signed the Device under duress 'compelled and treated almost as if they were prisoners'[1]. Bedford then, rather than acting out of sudden opportunism, had never wanted the succession altered. He signed the Device because Northumberland was in the superior position, backed by the king himself.

Several factors influenced Bedford's distaste for tampering with the succession. Mary's Catholicism did not distress the earl as it did committed Protestants like his own son. It has been consistently clear that Bedford's views on religion, which cannot be labelled simply Catholic or Protestant, were always strikingly pragmatic and Erastian. But in any case, he had already indicated his willingness to accept a conservative religious policy when, in October of 1549, he had supported Warwick's apparent religious conservatism. Moreover, in January 1550, as Warwick moved against the Catholics at court, the Imperial ambassador thought Bedford inclined to favour that group.[2] Not alarmed about Mary's religious views when he opposed the Device, Russell worried instead about the disputed succession and the prospect of civil war, the twin evils which would result from the Device. Henry .VIII had explicitly signified that Mary succeed to the throne should Edward have no heirs. Bedford wanted to comply with Henry's directive as the safest course for the nation at large.

Furthermore, Bedford and his wife had enjoyed a close relationship with Princess Mary, dating from the 1530s when Lady Russell served as maid to Mary.[3] In April 1550, Mary wrote to one of the Privy

House of Lords from 13 March through 30 March; *APC;* IV, 235-45 *and Journal of the House of Lords,* I, 434-42.

1   *Cal. S.P. Spain,* XI, 66-67, 70, 95.

2   *Ibid.,* X, 8.

3   For Anne Russell's relationship with Mary, see F. Madden, *Privy Purse Expenses of the Princess Mary* (London, 1831), pp.7, 51, 82, 97, 127-28, 155;

Councillors for a favour and called her correspondent her 'an[c]her nexte the kynge maiesty'. Bedford might well have been the intended recipient, who obviously enjoyed Mary's confidence, and the letter is in fact copied and catalogued at the Bedford Office in London.[1] No doubt Bedford's signature on the Device shook Mary's trust. Yet by 1554 her confidence in him was restored; she selected the earl to meet Philip in Spain and escort him and his large retinue back to England, a task of extreme importance in the queen's eyes and one very dear to her heart.[2]

Thus Bedford's position in June 1553 becomes explicable. Somewhat secure in his relationship with Mary, not particularly troubled by the religious issue, and loyal by nature to the Tudor dynasty, he found the Device a distasteful instrument. But Northumberland acted out of strength and with Edward's support. Therefore Bedford, like Shrewsbury, Cheyney, Arundel, Winchester, and the others, signed the altered will. Having once given his signature, he hesitated. Whereas Pembroke, Winchester, and Arundel were ready to desert Northumberland, Bedford fell back upon his instincts, which always counselled cautious, careful action. The fact that Francis Russell had been entrusted with Windsor Castle seems to have increased his sense of responsibility.[3] When he finally agreed on 19 July to accept Mary, he acted not in isolation but with the Council as a group. By this time, Mary had collected a considerable following on her own, and further compliance under Northumberland would have meant civil war. Once again, Bedford hit upon a happy combination of self-interest and principle. Far from accepting under duress a disagreeable fate, he agreed to the decision of 19 July and would have preferred it originally to the Device.

During the first year of the new reign, Bedford was an unobtrusive member of Mary's expanded Privy Council, one of several Edwardians whom the queen appointed.[4] Mary had a number of reasons to include

---

L.P., XIII(ii), 1280(f. 55); Cal. S.P. Spain, IX, 88. See also L.P., XI, 225.

1 For the original, see BL, Cotton MSS., Vesp.,F. XIII, fol. 280. It is signed 'your lovying assured frend duryng my lief'. Historians have recognized close ties between Bedford and Mary. See Strickland, Lives of the Queens of England, II, 496 and E.H. Harbison, Rival Ambassadors at the Court of Queen Mary (Princeton, 1940), p. 40.

2 BL, Sloane MS. 4149, fols. 35-37 and Cotton MSS., Vesp., F. III, fol. 23.

3 Froude's suggestion (History of England), VI, 35-36) rings true. Russell clearly worried about his son's position in the initial months of Mary's reign. See below, pp. 97-100.

4 Bedford was sworn in as councillor on 29 July; APC, IV, 419. The patent

on her Council men who had served her brother. Some such as Arundel had worked on her behalf since Edward's death; Bedford represented the traditional supporters of the dynasty. Furthermore, Bedford and fellow magnates such as Shrewsbury, Pembroke, and Westmorland dominated important segments of the realm. Their support would give Mary some sense of security. And as a group, these councillors possessed experience and ability. clear assets to the new government.

By the time that Mary had rewarded her servants, restored her friends, and reinstated the Edwardians, the Council's membership had grown to over forty, a group too unwieldy to govern effectively. Not all the councillors attended meetings regularly, however, and in fact, no more than twenty-seven ever attended any one session.[1] Moreover, the Marian Council was not as bedevilled by factionalism as historians once thought and the reports of the Imperial ambassador imply. Differences there were, especially between Lord Chancellor Gardiner and Lord Paget, but Gardiner was often isolated from the other Catholics on the active Council. Bedford was associated with the *politiques,* who followed Paget's leadership; these 'new men', experienced politicians and civil servants, were anxious to preserve their monastic spoils and more likely to think in terms of national interest and self-interest than religious principle.

Although Bedford's name figures in proceedings at court, he was initially neither as active nor as influential as he had been during Edward's reign. In November he joined a contingent of nobles, councillors, and Members of Parliament that petitioned Mary to choose an English husband.[2] But the prime English candidate, the young Edward Courtenay, Earl of Devonshire, could not have been that attractive in Bedford's eyes. The Courtenay family, after all, were his rivals in the west, and he would not have relished their advancement. That consideration, reinforced by a generous pension from the Imperial ambassador, helped convert Bedford to the Spanish match favoured by Paget.[3] Yet when Paget advised the emperor to write to

---

naming him keeper of the privy seal is dated 3 November; *Cal. Pat. Rolls, Mary*, I, 208.

1 G.A. Lemasters, 'The Privy Council in the Reign of Queen Mary I', unpublished dissertation, Cambridge University, 1972, pp.25-29. The information in this paragraph is derived from Lemasters' work, which revises the traditional view of an inefficient Council.

2 *Cal. S.P. Spain*, XI, 363.

3 Bedford's pension of 1,000 crowns was not atypical. Harbison estimates that the Imperial ambassador Renard gave or promised some 35,000 crowns

seven councillors to open the marriage negotations, he omitted Bedford's name. Later in December when councillors drafted the marriage treaty, the lord privy seal was absent from their ranks.[1]

Bedford took no meaningful part in the conduct of government affairs through 1553.[2] His health may have accounted for his passivity, but during the next year, at the age of sixty-nine, he was to manage a strenuous journey to Spain. More probably, he deliberately assumed an unobtrusive profile in 1553 in order to gain time. The queen needed reassurance of his loyalty. Not only had he himself supported Northumberland's Protestant policies, but also his son Francis openly opposed Mary during the accession crisis and was placed under house arrest. Not until November was Francis Russell pardoned, no doubt through his father's influence.[3] Under such circumstances Bedford naturally tread cautiously.

Only temporarily, in the early months of 1554, did Bedford assume a central, activist role on Mary's Council. Wyatt's rebellion provided him ample opportunity to demonstrate at least his own loyalty. Mary was instrumental in saving her own throne by courageously appealing to her subjects in person but, in the end, her government owed its survival to the great secular peers. Pembroke, Bedford, Clinton, and Paget held London Bridge against Wyatt's army and thereby broke the back of the rebellion in early February.[4] Bedford found himself back at the heart of government; he was named to a commission of the ordnance and served during the first week by March as one of six members of an inner Council created by Paget to promote efficiency and minimize Gardiner's influence.[5]

But such active participation in the Council's affairs did not last.

(£10,000) before Philip's arrival in England. Harbison, *Rival Ambassadors,* pp.341-42; *Cal. S.P. Spain,* XIII, 315.

1  *Cal. S.P. Spain,* XI, 270, Gammon, *Statesman and Schemer,*p.196.

2  Harbison, *Rival Ambassadors,* p.145, note 15. Bedford attended Privy Council meetings sporadically.

3  *Cal. S.P. Spain,* XI, 94; Strype, *Ecclesiastical Memorials,* III(i), 98; *Cal. Pat. Rolls, Mary,* I, 282.

4  Stow, *Annales,* pp.618-21; John Gough Nichols, ed., *The Chronicle of Queen Jane and of Two Years of Queen Mary and especially of the Rebellion of Sir Thomas Wyatt written by a Resident in the Tower, Camden Society,* XLVIII (London, 1850), p.39. Pollard, *The History of England from the Accession of Edward VI,* p.109.

5  *APC,* IV, 397 and Harbison, *Rival Ambassadors,* p.145, note 15. For a full explanation of Paget's reforms and reorganization scheme, see Lemasters, 'The Privy Council in the Reign of Queen Mary I', pp.163 ff. Bedford's commission was one of several created for specific administrative purposes.

Paget soon specified that the inner six include Arundel, Petre, Gardiner, Sir Robert Rochester, Bishop Thirlby, and himself. The great peers like Pembroke, Shrewsbury, and Bedford were excluded although they might attend occasional sessions. Hence the decline in Bedford's role on the Council, a decline begun in 1553, now resumed; his name appears on only a few routine commissions.[1] Of course, the earl was physically removed from the Council during much of the last year of his career, travelling on behalf of the royal marriage from April through July,[2] then growing ill by January. At any rate, he had little cause to lament his diminished participation in Privy Council matters. His prestige remained high; his lands were intact; his son, implicated in Wyatt's rebellion, had again been pardoned;[3] he himself still held one of the great offices of state; and he continued to perform work for the crown.

Now in his last important official act, Bedford led a deputation to Spain on behalf of Mary's marriage, in many ways a most appropriate closing for his long years of service to the crown. He went as personal envoy of his monarch, a role in which he had been comfortable since the 1520s. The prince whom he went to greet was the grandson of that archduke whom he had met in Dorset in 1506, a meeting that had in fact inaugurated his career. The marriage treaty had already been signed and publicly proclaimed in England. Bedford and his companion, Lord Fitzwalter, were to see it ratified under the emperor's seal and returned to England, a formality since the emperor had already agreed to its provisions.[4] Bedford's chief responsibility lay in making arrangements for Philip's trip to England. The task was not small, for the Spanish prince eventually sailed with a retinue of 600 men in a fleet of over one hundred ships. Planning Philip's itinerary, Bedford wanted the retinue to disembark at Southampton. The other alternatives, Plymouth and Exeter, would mean expenses for Bedford's clients and friends in the west and, very probably, danger for Philip since the marriage was extremely unpopular in the west. But Bedford and

---

1  *Cal. S.P. Spain*, XII, 168-69; *Cal. Pat. Rolls, Mary*, I, 302, 381.

2  Russell's date of departure is uncertain. He ceased attending Council meetings on 28 February; *APC*, IV, 401 ff. He was present, however, when Parliament opened on 5 April although absent by the next day; *Journal of the House of Lords*, I, 447 ff. He had been awaiting supplies and ships during the month of March; *Cal. S.P. Spain*, XII, 141, 149, 156, 177.

3  *Cal. S.P. Spain*, XII, 140; *Cal. Pat. Rolls, Mary*, II, 204.

4  Charles L. Kingsford, ed., 'Two London Chronicles form the Collections of John Stow', *Camden Miscellany*, XII, Camden Society, Third Series, XVIII (London, 1910), p.31; BL, Sloane MS. 4149, fols. 35-37 and Cambridge University, Gg. 5.36, fols. 84-85.

Fitzwalter warned that Philip suffered from sea-sickness and advised that Plymouth be prepared in case he should want to land prematurely.[1]

Bedford's efforts succeeded; the company landed at Southampton on 19 July. There the lord privy seal received further instructions from the anxious queen written in her own hand. Bedford was to explain to Philip the state of the realm and 'in all thynges he shall aske your advyse to decl[are] your opinion as becommeth a faythfull counceyllour to do'.[2] The old earl had no trouble with such directives. All went according to plan, and on 25 July the royal marriage took place:

> when it came to the gift of the queen, it was asked who showd give her. Then the Marquis of Winchester, the earles of Derby, Bedford and Pembroke, gave her highnes, in the name of the realm.[3]

After the marriage arrangements, references to Bedford become increasingly meagre. When Parliament convened in November 1554, he was named, as usual, a trier of petitions and was chosen in December to sit on two parliamentary committees. But his attendance was irregular and, like his presence at the formal sessions of the Privy Council, even this activity ceased in mid-January.[4] From then until his death in March, he suffered from bad health.

Bedford's will, drawn up in February, bequeathed the standard amount for charitable purposes and provided for his servants and his sister Thomasine. His wife and son inherited the great bulk of his goods and lands. As long as Lady Bedford lived, she had ultimate authority over all property; Francis was 'not to meddle' with his half of the land without her consent.[5] In this way Bedford transferred the whole of his estate into jointure. Jointures were usually spared in forfeitures for treason. Bedford had been 'greatly perturbed' over his son's involvement in Wyatt's rebellion, and he evidently wished to protect

---

1 Tytler, *England under the Reigns of Edward VI and Mary*, II, 410-11.

2 BL, Cotton MSS., Vesp., F. III, fol. 23.

3 Nichols, *The Chronicle of Queen Jane and of Two years of Queen Mary*, p.169.

4 *Journal of the House of Lords*, I, 464, 472. *APC* are inaccurate here. According to the index, Bedford's attendance stops on 14 January 1555 (V, 88) and then resumes the following year (V, 217) when in fact he died in March. In November Bedford stood as godfather with Prince Philip to the infant Philip Sidney, grandson of the late Northumberland. See Malcolm William Wallace, *The life of Sir Philip Sidney* (New York, 1967), p.12. Philip's father, Sir Henry Sidney, had accompanied Bedford on his journey to Spain. I thank Dr. Daniel Traister for drawing this matter to my attention.

5 F. 5 Ketchyn; for copy and probate of Bedford's will, see DRO, W 1258, GE 1/10.

the estate against the consequences of his son's political and religious ardour.[1]

The earl died on 14 March 1555 at the age of seventy in his house on the Strand in London. Although he had left instructions that his funeral be a modest and simple affair without 'vayne glorie', the passing of such an important figure of state demanded pomp and ceremony. Three hundred horses, all black, marched in the funeral procession on 20 March. The body was carried from the Bedford home in London to Buckinghamshire for burial on the Chenies estate. *En route,* greeted by priests at each town, the procession dispensed alms. Once at Chenies, on the day after the burial, the Dean of St. Paul's made 'a godly sermon' and the funeral ended with a great feast.[2] A year later Bedford's widow had a new chapel built to commemorate her husband's brial site and house his tomb, itself a work of art carved in alabaster, probably by an Italian craftsman, a fitting memorial for a sixteenth-century noble of Bedford's wealth and status.[3]

Bedford's career thus closed with a lavishness and splendour that only heightens all the more his modest gentry origins. The Chenies estate where he was buried represented only a fraction of the landed wealth that he had accumulated during his lifetime. For future generations, the Bedford name would be associated not so much with Chenies nor with his Devon holdings as with Woburn and valuable sites in London, acquisitions made late in his career. Indeed Bedford's property lay scattered throughout the counties of England. He had used all the standard means to augment his holdings (marriage, gifts, purchases, leaseholds) with striking success. Serving his government well, he had been well served in return. In these lands lay his greatest legacy, the other side of his public career, the establishment of a great family fortune.

1  *Cal. S.P. Spain,* XII, 146. I am grateful to Professor Russell for discussing with me the implication of the jointure provision.

2  Henry Machyn, *The Diary of Henry Machyn, Citizen and Merchant Taylor of London,* ed., J.G. Nichols, Camden Society, XLII (London, 1848), pp. 83-84; Strype, *Ecclesiastical Memorials,* III(i), 355.

3  BRO, Box 262, [Thomson], 'Chenies, The Chapel'. Thomson compares the sculpture to Torrigiano's tomb of Henry VII at Westminster.

# 6

## THE BEDFORD WEALTH

Spectacular economic achievement is frequently associated with the new nobility of Henry VIII. These peers rose within a lifetime from the ranks of the gentry or the middle class to the status of great magnate; they performed loyally for the Tudor dynasty at a time when compensation in land was readily available. The Russells fit, indeed they helped to create, the stereotype. During the reign of Henry VIII, John Russell's grandfather supposedly had an income worth £40 *per annum.* Yet Russell bequeathed to his son Francis, the second Earl of Bedford, lands whose yearly rental recipts exceeded £2,000.[1]

As Russell acquired his estate, leased, sold or rented lands, he engaged in hundreds of transactions. Fortunately, enough sources survive — particulars from the court of augmentation, deeds, leases, feet of fine records, licences to alienate — to answer a variety of questions about his activities on the land market. His transactions naturally fall into three categories: acquisitions, sales, and management. The historian interested in the progressive expansion of the Bedford landed wealth will want to trace the growth of the estate chronologically. Concerned with the machinations behind the acquisitions, with the techniques employed to accumulate the land, he will want also to classify and analyse the property as gifts, purchases, leases, inheritance or marital gains. Alternatively, those curious about economic issues or sixteenth-century agriculture will want to examine Russell's property as economic units in terms of geographic patterns and rental policies. This study cannot exhaust all these approaches but incorporates several of them to draw as comprehensive a picture as possible. Russell's acquisitions are first chronicled through 1539, formative years when he slowly increased his holdings and then received the great Tavistock grant. His property transactions during this initial period were important and versatile, yet still modest enough for chronological treatment. His acquisitions after 1539 are classified and discussed by categories, illustrating the different methods used to expand holdings. Finally, some of Russell's practices as a landlord, in particular his rental policies, are considered.

---

1 Helen Miller, 'The Tudor Peerage, 1485-1547', M.A. Thesis, University of London, 1951, p.124; Lawrence Stone, *The Crisis of the Aristocracy* (Oxford, 1965), Appendix VIII, p.760.

Russell's first property, his inheritance, lay primarily in the county of Dorset; the manors of Berwick, Chaldon Herring, and Blintfield, a house at Dorchester, some tenements in Weymouth, land in Stour Provost. His patrimony also included two tracts in Somerset: the manor of Moreton and land called Shitterton. James Russell had bequeathed the use of these latter holdings to his wife and given his son reversionary rights. John, however, never came into actual possession of the Somerset property, for in 1509, at the age of twenty-four, he sold his rights there for £200. Within the next decade, additional pieces of the patrimony were alienated, but Berwick and Chaldon Herring remained in his possession.[1] Situated a few miles from the Dorset coast, north of the village of Swyre, Berwick manor was not far from the port of Weymouth. Its stone house was small but pleasant, with five hundred acres of pasture and arable land. Russell's uncle may have managed its affairs. Russell himself never spent much time there although he seems not to have leased the manor until the end of his life.[2]

The first turning point in the history of Russell's land acquisitions came with his marriage in 1526 to Anne, the daughter and heiress of Sir Guy Sapcote.[3] Chenies in Buckinghamshire now became the Russells' countryside residence. The house was two stories high, not grand but comfortably large, surrounded by attractive grounds close to the village green. Located in the southeast of the county, it lay within convenient riding distance from Westminster, probably its main attraction to Russell.[4] He took an immediate interest in the property and within four years had added an extensive south wing to the house. So much of the original fifteenth-century structure was rebuilt that according to John Leland 'little or nothing of it . . . remayneth ontranslated'. The brickwork and the chimneys on the south wing resembled that of Hampton Court, and the same workmen may have participated in both projects.[5] Unfortunately, little is known about the interior of Chenies. An inventory for the year 1585 survives, but by then Francis

1   PRO, C 142/40/28, C 142/40/48, Wards 2/36/142. I have relied upon Thomson for the history of these early holdings; see *Family Background*, pp.201-11 and *Two Centuries of Family History*, pp.147-48, 185.

2   Thomson, *Family Background*, pp.201-2, 210, 248.

3   See above, p. 14.

4   Thomson, *Family Background*, pp.83, 86-87; see also, Thomson's typed report, 'Chenies, The House', BRO, Box 262.

5   John Leland, *The Itinerary of John Leland In or About the Years 1535-1543*, ed. Lucy Toulmin Smith (London, 1907), I, 105; Thomson, *Family Background*. p.88.

Russell had made changes and additions. One interesting item clearly dated from the early period: in the large bedroom on the ground floor stood a 'great' enormous, royal bed, decorated with Henry VIII's arms. In fact two such royal beds were kept at Chenies, probably dating from October 1542 when the king and his entourage attended a Privy Council session there.[1]

While Russell enjoyed and enlarged Chenies, he also engaged in legal procedures to protect Anne's title to the property. In the late fifteenth century, the manor, then called Isenhamstead, had belonged to Sir John Cheyney. When Cheyney and his wife died with no heirs, the manor and advowson were bequeathed to their niece, Anne Russell's grandmother. But in 1516 another John Cheyney, descendant of the original owner, brought Anne and her first husband to court. Although a jury settled the matter in Anne's favour, Cheyney did not accept the decision, for in 1532 Russell asked for an exemplification of the earlier verdict. Not until 1560 was the dispute completely settled, this time more to the Cheyneys' satisfaction. Francis, the second earl, received confirmation of his title to the property after paying a monetary award for the advowson.[2]

After his marriage, Russell owned substantial holdings in the adjacent counties of Buckinghamshire, Northamptonshire, and Huntingdonshire. When his wife's jointure was included, his annual income approached £400.[3] The estate experienced no dramatic growth for the next decade. Royal grants to Russell during this period tended to be stewardships and lordships of parks, manors, or woods, not outright gifts of lands.[4] For his own part, Russell seems to have purchased lands worth £16.10s. in the counties of Lincoln and Leicester and otherwise leased properties.[5] Not until the late 1530s did the estate again experience impressive growth. Henry's pleasure at the birth of his heir prompted the king to new acts of generosity, and Russell, by then comptroller of the royal household and Privy

---

1   Thomson, *Family Background,* pp.96, 102 ff.; cf. *L.P., XVI,* 1287. Thomson inaccurately claims that Henry never visited Chenies.

2   For legal proceedings, see PRO, C 1/670/11; BRO, Calendar (Transcripts), I, 438. The story of the manor is presented in Thomson, *Family Background.* p.85 and in William Page, ed. *Victoria History of the County of Buckingham* (London, 1925), II, 200-1.

3   See above, p. 15. Note Amersham grant, a wedding gift from the king; above, p. 14, n. 3.

4   E.g., *L.P.,* IV(iii), 6751(12); VIII, 149(21).

5   *Ibid.,* V, 978(19); *Bridges, The History and Antiquities of Northamptonshire,* II, 406. By 1539 Russell had in his possession some holdings whose date and mode of acquisition is not clear; PRO, E 315/418.

Councillor, received his share of gifts. A grant in May 1538 was derived primarily from the property of the late Duke of Buckingham: reversionary rights to the manors of Haverell, Hersham, and Heylon in Suffolk and outright possession of Lamewath manor in Yorkshire as a fee simple. In June, the king granted Russell manors in Lincoln and Northamptonshire from the lands of the attainted John Hussey. These grants of 1538, worth £71.16s.8d., were but a prelude to the Tavistock gift, still a year away.[1]

By 1539 Russell's career had reached the end of its initial phase. During this thirty year period, he had made no major purchases but had instead depended upon his inheritance, his marriage, and gifts from the crown for the expansion of his estate. He had sold or alienated very little of his lands.[2] It is hardly surprising that he had moved cautiously and conservatively on the land market, for such prudence also characterized his political career. Other factors accounted for his restrained behaviour during the initial stage of his acquisitions. He had limited resources of his own to invest. Monastic dissolution had not yet reached its peak, and the market had yet to be infused with the stimulant of new lands. (As Russell's own acquisitions demonstrate, most of the royal grants were still derived from the lands of attainted lords.)    Finally, at this point in his career, Russell may well have possessed a rather modest self-image and consequently rather modest ambitions. His total yearly income in 1539, including fees and annuities, was approximately £550 , a respectable showing but still the result of three decades of service.[3] In all these respects, the Tavistock grant and other rewards in 1539 marked a significant change, transforming Russell's situation and behaviour. He left the ranks of the upper gentry to become a noble and soon thereafter began to purchase and lease manors on an extensive basis. By the 1540s his life style changed, his resources increased, and his economic activities assumed new directions.

In one stroke in July 1539, the crown alienated some thirty thousand acres worth over £930 to Lord Russell. In Fuller's words, 'a good share of the golden showre of Abbey Lands fell into his lap . . .'.[4]  Unlike most of the monastic lands in Devon, which were sold in small parcels

---

1  Suffolk lands were already in Anne Russell's use. See above, p. 30, 1. Unless otherwise indicated, all values date from 1539 (PRO, E 315/418).

2  Russell enfeoffed lands from the manor of Chenies to prevent feudal obligations should he die while his heir was a minor; PRO. CP 25(2)/3/14, fol. 43.

3  See above, p. 30.  Valor of 1539 does not specify every holding and omits some leaseholds.

4  Fuller, *Worthies of England* (I), 281. Hoskins estimates acreage in *Devon and its People*, p.79.

to resident gentry, the Tavistock grant enriched and introduced a new landlord to the county. Although requiring an annual reserved rent of £284.5s., the grant more than doubled his assets. The gift had qualifications. Rather than representing the usual tenth, the rent actually represented one-quarter of the property's value. And the land was given in two parcels, to be held by the service of two knights' fee.[1] Nevertheless, the grant was the most generous gift that Russell ever received from Henry VIII; more than any other act, it illustrates the debt that this new noble owed to the Tudor dynasty.

Russell acquired the site and church of Tavistock Abbey, the hundred and borough of Tavistock, the manors of Hurdwick, Burrington, Werrington, Cornwood, Plymstock, Denbury, Christow, and Cowick – in all, twenty manors in Cornwall, Devon, and Somerset. The king did exclude parts of the Tavistock estate from the grant but gave in their stead the manor and rectory of Blackawton, Dominican property in Exeter, the rectories of Dunkeswell and Awliscombe, and the site of Dunkeswell Abbey, itself some six thousand acres. The gifts also included some seventeen advowsons and thirteen parish churches. Accompanying grants both in July and September further ensured Russell's position as leading aristocrat in the western provinces by appointing him to many offices formerly held by Henry Courtenay, the late Marquis of Exeter. In October he again received land outright, this time the Courtenay manor of Caryfytzpan in Somerset.[2]

Since Russell intended to keep Chenies as his country home, he consequently chose for his lodging in the west a town house, the Dominican property in Exeter. Formerly the house of the Black Friars, it was located just behind the Cathedral and stood two to three stories high, adorned with impressive gables. It included a great hall, domestic offices and kitchens on its ground floor and private family rooms upstairs.[3] After 1540 and the demise of the Council of the West, Russell's visits there grew infrequent. In these circumstances he saw no need to retain unused the large extravagant Tavistock buildings, which he leased to Dorothy, Lady Mountjoy.[4]

---

1  *L.P.,* XIV(i), 1354(13); DRO, W 1258, GE 1/3. Grant is printed in Youings, *Devon Monastic Lands: Calendar of Particulars,* pp.5-7; summarized in Youings, 'The Disposal of Monastic Property', pp.171-72 and Finberg, *Tavistock Abbey,* pp.268-70.  Note that the figure of £930, excluded advowsons and woods.

2  See above, p. 65, n.3 and *L.P.,* XIV(ii), 435(17). Russell was named keeper of Exmoor Forest with wages, rents. herbage and pannage there.  In return he paid the crown £46.13s.4d. yearly: DRO, W 1258, GE 1/7.

3  D. Portman, *Exeter Houses 1400-1700* (Torquay, 1966), p.37.

4  DRO, L 1258, I, 1/a. Finberg suggests that Russell negotiated the lease

A far different fate awaited the buildings of Dunkeswell Abbey, also part of Henry's grant. In November 1539 Russell made a bargain of sale with John Haydon (alias Heydon), a western resident and a colleague at Lincoln's Inn. Haydon was allowed to tear down the abbey buildings and given rights to all glass, iron, timber, stone, and lead found on the premises, excepting only that glass and iron of the cloister already sold to Russell's servant Thomas Ketyll. Haydon paid a total of £28 and was given ten years to complete his work of plunder. But Russell carefully protected his own interests: 'if any treasure chaunce or happen to be founde yn and aboute the said church . . . then all and eny of such treasure shall be equally and yndyfferently dyvyded . . .'. And he required £40. in advance to enforce this stipulation. The Dunkeswell transaction shows him at least temporarily as a parvenu landlord participating in that economic exploitation so often associated with the Reformation.[1]

By 1540 he was in a position to take advantage of the new availability of monastic lands. He now owned extensive property in both the home counties and the west country. He had at least three homes       at Chenies, in Exeter, and a new large house in London on the Strand.[2] He was lord president in the west, an important Privy Councillor, and in 1540 he assumed the post of lord admiral. In this situation he could afford some risk and willingly engaged in land transactions on a scale which he had hitherto avoided. He made purchases and then alienated several of them. Some he probably sold to finance subsequent purchases and meet reserved rent payments. For five years he was especially active in the Henrician land market.

He bought his first major acquisition from the crown in 1540: the manor of Clopton Hall in Suffolk and that of Aston Abbots in Buckinghamshire, two counties where he already possessed property. The new holdings came from the monastic lands of Bury and St. Albans. In the case of Aston Abbots, he purchased not only the manor but also the parish church and its tithes, the advowson, and vicarage. The grant was valued at £52.1s.5½d. *per annum* after the tenth or

because he was short of cash; *Tavistock Abbey,* p.271. While Russell no doubt welcomed new income, he was not so poor that he refrained from major purchases. Youings provides an explanation for the lease when she cites the extravagence of the monastic residence; 'The Disposal of Monastic Property', pp.270-72.

1   DRO, W 1258, G 5/4. The indenture is printed in G.H. Radford, 'Travistock Abbey', *Transactions of the Devonshire Association,* 46 (1914), 147-49. Finberg suggests Russell's need for ready cash motivated the speculative deal; *Travistock Abbey,* p.270.

2   See above, p. 29, n. 3.

reserved rent was subtracted and priced at £1,041.9s.2d., a twenty-years purchase rate; Russell was expected also to pay the tenth of £5.15s.10d. as an annual rent to the crown. The whole procedure was perfectly standard. The court of augmentations valued and surveyed the property in February; the latter patent authorizing the sale was issued on 14 March.[1]

Russell next negotiated an extensive land exchange with the crown, a common procedure in this sixteenth-century market. Royal grants often included diverse and widespread holdings, and in this situation owners found advantage and convenience in exchanging land deeds either with one another or with the crown on favourable terms. In July 1541 Russell restored part of the 1539 grant, particularly the site of Dunkeswell Abbey, to the king. In return he received a series of new holdings: Pedmore in Buckinghamshire; Finneshade, Eybury, and Kirby in Northamptonshire; Hough and Geston in Lincoln; messuages in Slawston and Othorpe, Leicestershire; Coldhall in Suffolk; and Fryer Pyes in Middlesex.[2]

He embarked on a new and major series of purchases in June 1543. One transaction included Acton, a former monastic manor in Middlesex, and the manor of Westley in Suffolk, which Russell had been leasing since 1532. Both holdings were rated by the court of augmentations this time for twenty-one years. Acton included a reserved rent of £1.14s., was valued at £15.6s. *per annum,* and was priced at £321.6s. Westley required no tenth since it had not been monastic property. It was simply rated as £5.13s.4d., the annual rent that Russell had been paying, and priced at £119.[3] Shortly thereafter Russell initiated a second, even larger purchase which included the manors of Ingliscombe, Wydcombe, Laverton, and Westhamptree in Somerset, formerly owned by the Earl of Huntingdon. Like the manor of Westley, the holdings in Somerset required no reserved rent. They were valued at £60.9s. *per annum* and their purchase price amounted to £1,269.9s., or with

---

1   The main terms of the grant appear in the letter patent, *L.P.* XV, 436(71). The individual items and values appear in the particulars of the court of augmentations, PRO, E 318/19/951. I have corrected mathematical errors that appear in any of the pariticulars. The best explanation of the purchase procedure is Youings, *Devon Monastic Lands,* p.xii, xviii and 'The Terms of Disposal of the Devon Monastic Lands, 1536-58', *English Historical Review* 69 (January 1954), 21-24.

2   *L.P.,* XVI, 1056(60); PRO, E 318/19/952. See H. J. Habakkuk, 'The Market for Monastic Property, 1539-1603', *Economic History Review,* Second Series 10, no. 3 (April 1958), p.376 for discussion of land exchanges.

3   PRO, E 318/19/953.

woods £1,367.10s.2d.[1] The crown issued one letter patent in August
to cover all these sales, which cost Russell a total of £1,807.16s.2d.[2]
Although he was to pay the sum in instalments, the acquisitions of
1543 meant heavy financial obligations.

Yet Russell continued to invest in the land market. He completed a
joint purchase in June 1544 for lands in Middlesex and an advowson in
Leicestershire worth a total of £305.16s.5½d.[3] In July he paid a twenty
years' purchase rate of £135 for Ingliscombe parsonage in Somerset,
adding to properties he already possessed there.[4] Earlier, in March
1543, he had lodged a request with the court of augmentations for
holdings near Chenies in the parish of Watford, Hertfordshire which
had formerly belonged to the monastery of St. Albans. The purchase
price for the items was £120.5s. including woods. He also requested
the rate for some small farms in Buckinghamshire, formerly the
property of Medmenham monastery. The final sale would in addition
include the rectory of Watford, previously priced at £396 and certain
tithe rights in Watford. A twenty years rate was again used to determine
the price of individual items. For some reason, perhaps because Russell
lacked ready funds, the sale was delayed until September 1545. He
agreed to reserved rents and a purchase price of £520.5s and once
more paid the crown in instalments.[5]

Russell completed these extensive purchases in the first half of the
decade. Crown lands were already undervalued, but investors did not
necessarily perceive their advantageous position.[6] No evidence suggests
that Russell in particular received preferential treatment in the pricing
of any of his purchases. Together they cost him approximately £3,810
to say nothing of the reserved rents he annually paid the crown. His
name and position at court undoubtedly facilitated many of the
transactions, but here too the evidence of favouritism on the part of the
auditors is slight. The purchases represent a unique period in his landed
career, for after 1545, except for some fee farms, Russell ceased to buy

1  PRO, E 318/19/954.

2  *L.P.*, XVIII(ii), 241(5).

3  *Ibid.*, XIX(i), 812(42 and 114) and PRO, E 315/337, fol. 23. The grant was
issued jointly to Russell and Roger Clerk of Burton, Dorset.

4  PRO, E 318/19/958; E 315/337, fol. 37.

5  PRO, E 318/19/955-57; *L.P.*, XX(ii), 49(56). I have found two instalment
payments: March 1545 for £140.5s.9d. (E 315/338, fol. 5) and December 1546
for £307.4s.4d. (E 315/339, fol. 102).

6  See Habakkuk, 'The Market for Monastic Property', pp.374-76.

monastic property from the crown.[1] Needless to say, the end of active purchases hardly meant that his acquisitions ceased to grow. Heavy financial obligations in 1546 and then the crown's renewed generosity during Edward's reign probably explain why he discontinued large purchases after 1545.

Not only did Russell buy properties but he also leased them from the crown (see Table I). Indeed new leaseholds tended to coincide with his most active period of purchases, the early 1540s. Since rents were often lower on crown lands than their true value, leases were profitable ventures for the renter.[2] Russell chose counties where he already had interests or, as in the case of Restormel and Boconnoc, properties which he had earlier managed for the crown.

Still one other type of acquisition that came Russell's way deserves special attention, for it reveals how personal contacts and court pressure might influence the land market. The items in question, the manors of Bishop's Clyst and Bishop's Tawton, were not even crown lands but episcopal holdings under the jurisdiction of Bishop Veysey of Exeter. Veysey himself, having served as president of the Council of Wales, was one of the last of the political churchmen and accustomed to living in a style of wealth and luxury. Although he played the role of political prelate well, he proved too weak to defend his diocese and its episcopal property once the Reformation began. In his pleasant and affable way, he found it easier to yield than to resist the demands of the crown and simply tried to make terms as generous to himself as possible. By 1549 the thirty-two manors once belonging to the diocese had been reduced to three or four. By 1551 when Veysey was compelled to resign, the episcopal estate was worth only £500 instead of its former £1,566.14s.6d.[3]

---

1 Since the tenure of fee farms lasted perpetually, they can be considered the equivalent of purchases. (I am grateful to Professor Wallace MacCaffrey of Harvard University for discussing the tensure with me). Youings notes that fee farms were common during the reign of Edward VI; Youings, *Devon Monastic Lands*, p.xviii.

2 Joyce Youings, 'Landlords in England', *The Agrarian History of England and Wales*, general ed. H.P. R. Finberg, vol. IV, *1500-1640*, ed. Joan Thirsk (Cambridge, 1967), 348.

3 Rowse, *Tudor Cornwall*, pp.142-43, 292-93; MacCaffrey, *Exeter*, p.175; J.D. Mackie, *The Earlier Tudors* (Oxford, 1952), p.518. Hooker complained that under Veysey 'one of the best bishoprikes withyn this land is become one of the poorest .'. The Common-Place Book of John Vowell, alias Hooker, Exeter City Muniments, Book 51, Reel 68, fol. 96 in Widener Library Microfilm Collection. William Knight, Bishop of Bath and Wells, also gave away ecclesiastical wealth and here too Russell benefited. See Phyllis Hembry, *The Bishops of Bath and Wells, 1540-1640* (London, 1967), p.74.

## TABLE I: RUSSELL'S CROWN LEASEHOLDS AFTER 1539

| Date | Terms of Lease | Property | County |
|------|----------------|----------|--------|
| 1540 | 21 yrs. £31. *p.a.* | lands in Tarrant and Parva Crawford; demesne of Tarrant monastery; manor of Kayneston; manor of Wynterborne-Musterton; tithes | Dorset |
| 1542 | 21 yrs. £28. *p.a.* | lands, mines, buildings in park of Restormel, lately disparked; reversionary rights to castle of Restormel | Cornwall |
| 1542 | 21 yrs. £6. *p.a.* | site of park of Boconnoc | Cornwall |
| 1543 | 21 yrs. a) £18.13s.4d. b) 27s. | a) pannage b) stable, barn, etc. of the park of King's Langley | Herts. |
| 1543 | in conjunction with wardship Russell was allowed £52. for yearly expenses £19.6s. *p.a.* | property of the late Sir Richard Pollard; Forde Mansion; lands called Hanford in Devon; a grange in Cornwall | Devon and Cornwall |
| 1544 | 21 yrs. £5.8s.2d. *p.a.* | manor of Southwitholme free rents amounting to 12s. | Lincs. |

*Sources:* L.P., XVII, 220(98); XV, 1032(64b) or Addenda (ii), 1448; XVII, 1154(78 and 34); XVIII(i), 476(24); XVIII(ii), 241(8); XIX(i), 278(53). John Bridges suggests that Russell was also leasing Oundle monastery in Northamptonshire; see above, p. 103, n.5.

Resident gentry as well as servants at court profited from the alienation of these lands. Among them were Sir Thomas Speke, Sir Lewis Pollard, Sir Thomas Darcy, Sir Thomas Denys, Sir William Paget, and Lord Russell, who all increased their holdings at the expense of the diocese. During Henry's reign the bishop granted most of the property in the form of leases. Under Edward, however, lands were permanently alienated, for the Privy Council then demanded and received outright gifts for its clients.[1]

The lord privy seal took advantage of this situation to enhance his estate, yet also remained on friendly terms with the bishop. In 1539 when first sent into the western counties, Russell was solicitous about Veysey's health as well as anxious for his company.[2] At this time the bishop named Russell and his son Francis to serve as chief steward of all castles, honours, and manors in possession of the see. Veysey's choice was a natural one. The office of high steward normally went to a person with great landed interests in the southwest and had last been filled by Henry Courtenay. Russell served in this post just as he filled several others that had formerly been Courtenay's. Four years later he was appointed steward of all the lands and possessions of the Dean and Chapter of Exeter.[3]

The offices paid a nominal fee and may well have been a sinecure, a way for the bishop to gain influential friends.[4] But if such were Veysey's strategy, in this case it failed. His influential friend remained first and foremost a servant of the crown and showed no inclination to defend the episcopal lands. In 1543 King Henry asked Veysey to grant Crediton Park to Sir Thomas Denys. When the bishop hesitated, he earned a stern rebuke from his steward. Russell expressed amazement that Veysey had yet to comply with the king's request, for Henry was 'very earnest in it, and fully determined'. Russell hoped that there 'not apper any obstinace unto his highness thereyn in any behalf . . .'.[5]

Similar pressure from the crown persuaded Veysey to lease the Devonshire manors of Bishop's Clyst and Tawton to Russell himself in 1546. Russell agreed to pay a rent of £158.3s.5d. for Tawton and

---

1 Pill, 'The Diocese of Exeter', pp.324-34.

2 PRO, S.P. 1/146, fol. 253 and *L.P.*, XIV(i), 685.

3 DRO, W 1258, A 1/8; Pill, 'The Diocese of Exeter', pp.56-57.

4 Pill, 'The Diocese of Exeter', p.57.

5 Russell quoted in George Oliver, *The History of Exeter* (Exeter, 1821), p.73. Russell had formerly been Denys' house guest; see PRO, S.P. 1/146, fol. 253.

£36.14s.10d. for Clyst.[1] Although the lease was to run for fifty years, the lord privy seal managed to extend his control over this land soon thereafter. On 31 January 1548, he gained new terms which increased his period of tenure by thirty years. After the Western Uprising in 1549, when those who had aided the crown were liberally rewarded, Russell received a ninety-nine year lease from the Dean and Chapter of Exeter for the manor, advowson, tithes, and parsonage of Clyst Honiton at an annual rent of £13.10s.4d. A few months later in January, Russell accepted the manors of Bishop's Clyst and Tawton as an out-and-out gift.[2]

According to the terms of the latter grant, the Bishop of Exeter yielded to the Privy Council which in turn had acted upon its 'well beloved Councillor['s] . . humble suit'.[3] Like his earldom also granted in January, the gift was a reward for Russell's support of Warwick in the recent *coup d'état*. Thus, within a span of five years, the influence of the crown helped him to acquire first a leasehold, then ownership of two episcopal manors worth nearly £200. He had added some four thousand acres of arable land, three hundred acres of meadow, two thousand acres of pasture, and one hundred acres of wood to his estate.[4]

As distinct from the Tawton and Clyst grant, which represented gifts from the church, most of Russell's free land came directly from the crown and, with the important exception of the Tavistock grant, most came during the reign of Edward VI. Henry VIII in the final years of his reign gave Russell only standard rewards.[5] But once Edward succeeded to the throne, a far different mood prevailed. Whereas Henry had granted gifts sparingly and only for good reason, the nobles who controlled the government after 1547 practised little restraint in distributing crown lands. Free grants became rampant, and Russell's holdings reflected the change. Nonetheless, by sixteenth-century standards, Russell showed neither greed nor unscrupulous behaviour in accumulating his properties. The fifteen free manors which Russell collected during Edward's reign compare favourably with the

---

1   In a letter signed by stamp, February 1546, Veysey was told 'to lease the manors . . . for 50 years to my lord Privy Seal at the "used rent" '. *L.P.*, XXI(i). 301(31). The lease, granted on 1 March, also included two   advowsons in Cornwall. DRO, W 1258, A 1/9.

2   DRO, W 1258, A 1/10, G 4/1, A 1/12; *Cal. Pat. Rolls, Edw. VI*, III, 164.

3   DRO, W 1258, A 1/12, fol. 1.

4   *Ibid.*, A 1/14-16.

5   *L.P.*, XIX(i), 278(6) and 812(11).

acquisitions of several of his colleagues: Warwick gained eighty-eight manors; Somerset, sixty-three; Pembroke, fifty-one; Thomas Seymour, forty-eight; even St John, eighteen. Warwick's gifts in land during the six-year reign ran to nearly £2,000, three times the amount that Russell received.[1]

The lord privy seal was given only one free grant during Somerset's tenure of power, namely the manor and site of Woburn Abbey and the granges of Utcott Crawley and Whitley in Bedfordshire. The property was altogether worth £168.18s.½d., and Russell agreed to pay £68.18s.½d. as an annual fee-farm rent. Eventually the abbey became Russell's most famous acquisition, for in later generations Woburn housed the Bedford mansion. For Lord Russell himself, however, the site had little significance. Since Sir Francis Bryan held a lease of Woburn in 1547, the lord privy seal gained reversionary rights only and probably never enjoyed outright possession of the property.[2]

Protector Somerset tended to hoard the crown's spoils for himself, but the gifts once more flowed after Warwick's *coup d'état*. At the time of his earldom, Russell requested and received lands worth £339.13s.1d., for which he in turn rendered a yearly rent close to £40.[3] Next, in May 1552, he received 'land called le Covent Garden in Fields next Charing Crosse . . . upon the king's highway . . . called Strondway'. Valuable though this land would become in the future of London real estate, in 1552 it represented a small piece of the late Duke of Somerset's estate and had a modest yearly value of £5.6s.8d.[4] Russell's final grant in June 1553 was intended by Warwick to fortify Lady Jane's accession. The lands in question were valued at £74.5 3/4d. and Russell together with a colleague agreed to pay an annual rent of £12.[5]

1 Jordan, *Edward VI*, I, 116; Beer: *Northumberland*, p.186. Thomson agrees that 'there is nothing to show that he was among the more shameless of the beggars'; *Two Centuries of Family History*, p.176.

2 See above, p. 56, n.4 and Gladys Scott Thomson, 'Woburn Abbey and the Dissolution of the Monasteries', *Transactions of the Royal Historical Society*, Fourth Series 16 (1933), 147. Russell also acquired property in Buckinghamshire, but this transaction completed a land exchange inaugurated during the reign of Henry VIII.

3 PRO, E 318/24/1415; *Cal. Pat. Rolls, Edw. VI*, III, 43. Most noteworthy of the new holdings were the manor, park, and advowson of Boconnoc in Cornwall and the manor and park of Chumleigh in Devon; the house and site of Thorney monastery in Cambridgeshire; the manor, fair, and park of Oundle in Northampton. Some of this property Russell already leased.

4 *Cal. Pat. Rolls, Edw. VI*, IV, 298. The grant was in free socage. Russell already possessed a tenement and garden lying near Covent Garden.

5 PRO, E 318/25/1416; *Cal. Pat. Rolls, Edw. VI*, V, 281-83. There is a slight

Hereafter the Bedford estate ceased to expand. Once Queen Mary ascended the throne, the political climate changed. Monastic lands no longer served as spoils, and the crown ended its generoisity to councillors such as Bedford, who were closely associated with the previous reign. For his part, Bedford did not assume the initiative and resume purchases as he had during the 1540s. Old age seems to have limited his ambitions and activities at least on the land market.[1]

Bedford had collected acquisitions enough to relax in his final years. From the crown during Edward's reign, his free gifts amounted to nearly £479 and from the church close to £200. He had also acquired since the death of King Henry fee farms worth an additional £120 *per annum*. The geographic spread of his property had grown steadily more impressive. During the Henrician period he had owned manors, in orders of numbers, in Devon, Lincoln, Somerset, Dorset, Suffolk, Buckinghamshire, Northamptonshire, Hertfordshire, Cornwall, Berkshire, Huntingdonshire, and Yorkshire.[2] During Edward's reign he accumulated new and extensive holdings in Bedfordshire and Cambridgeshire while his lands also increased elsewhere, notably in Buckinghamshire, Somerset, and Middlesex. The Bedford influence was firmly entrenched in counties throughout the realm by the time of the first earl's death.

Like all other areas of Tudor history, the agricultural sphere contains its share of controversies. Disagreement and debate range over several issues: land speculation, agricultural techniques, the enclosure movement, the changing position of tenants, the role of new, perhaps improving landlords, the trend in rents and, subsuming all these questions, the old bugbear of capitalism. As a sixteenth-century landlord, Russell acted in several of the spheres now of interest to economic and agricultural historians. What were his policies once his lands were acquired? How much of his estate did he retain and how much did he re-sell for economic advantage in a time of inflation?

Property held by knight service, which included most former

discrepancy in the figures cited. The grant included holdings in Bellerica, Somerset; Camelton, Bedfordshire; Hopton, Hertfordshire; Boyton, Cornwall; Ludgarshall, Wiltshire. Most of the land was given in socage and granted jointly to Russell and Edmund Downing, gentleman.

1 New tenants bought reversionary rights to Bedford's crown leases during this period; *Cal. Pat. Rolls, Mary*, I, 335, 346-7.

2 Russell's manors have been tabulated in terms of geographic distribution for the Henrician years; Miller, 'The Tudor Peerage', Add. Appendix. Prior to any sales, the number of manors varied from twenty-six in Devon to one in Berkshire, Huntingdon, Cornwall, and Yorkshire.

monastic property, could be alienated or sold only by a royal licence obtained by a fine payable in chancery. During the course of his life, Russell purchased sixteen such licences. Although they reveal tendencies in his economic behaviour, unfortunately licences did not specify the purpose of alienation (resale, exchange, or creation of a use).[1] He obtained all but three of the licences during the years 1540-1545, the half-decade which coincided with his most active period of land purchases. Seven of them refer to purchased properties; five were meant for lands gained in exchanges; two refer to lands received as gifts, and two to fee farms. In fourteen cases he alienated holdings within one year, sometimes in a matter of weeks or even days, after he had acquired them.[2]

When transferring property, Russell's transactions reflected interests in the counties rather than his court connections. Occasionally, he dealt with an associate at court as when in 1548 he bought land from a fellow councillor, Sir William Paget.[3] In the west political and economic contacts were especially likely to merge. For example, in 1540 Russell transferred (probably sold) some holdings in Somerset to Sir John Horsey, then a colleague on the Council of the West.[4] But Horsey was also a member of the resident gentry, and in general, new holders were likely to be men residing in the county where the land was situated rather than political acquaintances. Documents from the feet of fines confirm this impression; so far as Russell's entries are concerned, the records are a catalogue of local names.[5]

According to the royal licences the recipients of Russell's lands included a merchant, at least four knights, and others who were either gentlemen or yeomen. These local figures recall R.H. Tawney's 'rising gentry', men who after 1540 improved their economic status at the expense of the older established peerage. The gentry controversy is not relevant to Russell's landed career, however. In some sense he himself stands in the camp of rising gentry, albeit for a generation

1  Conrad Russell, 'Land Sales 1540-1640: A Comment on the Evidence', *Economic History Review*, Second Series 25, no. 1 (April 1972), 117-19. I am grateful to Professor Russell for discussing with me ambiguities in the evidence

2  For licences, see *L.P.*, XV, 282(1), 733(31); XVI, 1056(74); XVII, 283(49), 361(2), 1154(39); XVIII(ii), 241(13 and 15); XIX(i), 278(76), 812(114); XX(i), 846(93); XX(ii), 1068(52); *Cal. Pat. Rolls, Edw. VI*, I, 359; V, 266, 267; PRO, CP 30/1120/9.

3  *Cal. Pat. Rolls. Edw. VI*, I, 332.

4  *L.P.*, XV, 282(1).

5  I have looked at the records for the years 1526-51; PRO CP 25(2). They include sales and the creation of uses to escape the possibility of wardship.

earlier than Tawney's men. Once he became a peer, he continued to acquire lands and at the same time sold property to members of classes below his own. The two processes occurred simultaneously and for the moment did not contradict one another.

No clear pattern emerges from the lands that Russell alienated. In one instance he apparently exchanged lands in Leicester in return for property near the family estate of Chenies but such consolidation was rare, and he did not hesitate on occasion to give up holdings in counties where he had extensive interests.[1] Evidence suggests that he may have engaged in speculation during the 1540s when he first had to pay large reserved rents. The manors of Aston Abbots, Clopton Hall, part of Ingliscombe, and Westley were alienated shortly after their purchase as were several lands gained in exchange.[2] Yet without resale prices and given the ambiguity among sales, exchanges, and uses, we can come to no definitive conclusions.

Even if Russell did engage in some speculative ventures, these episodes did not dominate his general economic behaviour. Instances of alienations were not unusually high for the amount of property coming into his hands. Like the majority of sixteenth-century landowners, he did not value land for its short-term capital gains and would have experienced difficulty in sustaining such gains in the Henrician land market. Paradoxically the opportunity for serious profit was more likely to befall the man who held onto his property than the speculator who looked for quick returns. Certainly in Russell's case, wealth and status derived from the property he retained not that he sold.[3]

But what then of the rents he charged, the leases he issued, and the profits he saw on those holdings which he retained? The old view propagated by Tawney looked with disfavour upon new landlords like Russell who, once enriched with monastic lands, allegedly set out to maximize gains on their investments no matter what the social cost. Tawney's view of the ambitious landlord intent upon commercialization has by now been effectively modified or challenged on a number of different grounds.[4] Where leases were already in effect, rents in fact

---

1  PRO, CP 25(2)/3/16, fol. 109 and CP 25(2)/24/154, fol. 25.

2  See esp. *L.P.* XV, 733(31); PRO, CP 30/1120/9; *L.P.*, XVIII(ii), 241(13 and 15).

3  See Youings, 'Landlords in England', pp.351-53; Habakkuk, 'The Market for Monastic Property', pp.377-80; Slavin, *Politics and Profit*, p.201.

4  For Tawney's argument, see *The Agrarian Problem in the Sixteenth Century*, ed. Lawrence Stone, pb ed. (New York, 1967). For revisionist arguments, see Eric Kerridge, *Agrarian Problems in the Sixteenth Century and After* (London,

lagged behind the prices of farm products, making the century a period of prosperity for the cultivator, that is the tenant. For new takings or lands with new leases, rents actually doubled in the first half of the century, primarily through increased fines.[1] But even in this instance, as Russell's case illustrates, the landlord's economic behaviour was limited by socio-economic pressures and the force of local custom.

Leaseholders by indentures were much less common in sixteenth-century England than customary tenants who comprised perhaps two-thirds of the renter-class.[2] The customary tenant occupied land at his lord's will according to the custom of the manor and was most often a copyholder by the late Tudor period. In the west some three-quarters of all tenants fell in the copyhold category. Yet even there leasehold by indenture grew more popular during the course of the century as an alternative to customary tenure, and the leaseholder had been traditionally well represented on some manors. As early as 1486 on the Tavistock Abbey manor of Werrington, for example, the fifty-four leaseholders far outnumbered the fifteen customary tenants.[3] In Tawney's mind, the emergence of the lease by indenture over the copyhold was a victory for capitalistic ownership at the expense of an older paternal feudal relationship. But customary tenancies themselves might include arbitrary fines and were not always free of exploitation while the lease by indenture offered attractions to both the tenant and the landowner. A leaseholder enjoyed some long-term security. He was more likely to make improvements on the land and thus spare the landlord the expense of ploughing capital back into his property.[4]

Leaseholders in the west made three distinct kinds of payment to their landlord: an annual rent, a heriot, and an entry fine. The rents could vary greatly within a single manor, depending upon the date of

1969) and 'The Movement of Rent, 1540-1640', *Economic History Review*, Second Series 6, no. 1 (August 1953), 16-34; Joan Thirsk, *Tudor Enclosures* (1959; rpt, London, 1967); A.R. Bridbury, Sixteenth-Century Farming', *Economic History Review*, Second Series 27, no. 3 (August 1974), esp. pp. 539-44, 553-56. Kerridge presents a general revisionist statement; Thirsk emphasizes demographic pressures while Bridbury minimizes the degree of innovation during the Tudor period.

1   Kerridge, 'Movement of Rent', pp.26-29. See also Peter Bowden, 'Agricultural Prices, Farm Profits, and Rents', *Argrarian History of England and Wales*, IV, 675, 679-80, 694-95.

2   Tawney, *The Agrarian Problem*, p.24.

3   W.G. Hoskins, *Devon* (London, 1954), p.90. See also J.E. Kew, 'The Land Market in Devon, 1536-1558', unpublished dissertation, University of Exeter, 1967, pp.90-91.

4   Bowden, 'Agricultural Prices', p.684.

the lease and value of the land farmed. The heriot was a death duty and on Tavistock property was usually specified as the best beast on the farm, a charge that kept pace with inflation. The entry fine was paid, often for reversionary rights, whenever a new lease was negotiated, and its importance as well as its value shot upwards as the century progressed. Landlords used the entry find rather than annual rental payments to compensate for the cost of inflation. Hence after 1550 rentals alone no longer give an accurate reflection of the true value of property. By then the crown, itself a conservative landlord, charged entry fines four or five times the annual rent, a fourfold increase since the 1530s. To determine the real price paid for the use of the land, we must include the annual rent, the entry fine, and even the interest lost on the entry fine, which was actually an advance premium payment.[1]

This question of leases and rents affords the most useful avenue to investigate Russell's policies as landlord. Adequate records for a study of the daily administration of his estate have not survived, but a series of leases by indenture is available from some of the Tavistock manors, lands in Russell's possession for sixteen years and a significant portion of the estate. Special attention has been given Hurdwick and Werrington, two manors where leaseholders were numerous. The evidence reveals trends in rents and entry fines and provides valuable information in reconstructing Russell's profile as landlord.

A survey of over eighty monastic indentures indicates that Tavistock Abbey in its last seventy years did not deviate from rental practices then common in the west.[2] Families leasing during the reign of Edward IV remained on the land during the reigns of Henry VII and Henry VIII. Until 1520 most leases tended to run for forty years, but thereafter they were usually shortened to two or three lives. (A life was considered the equivalent of seven years. The lessee, his wife, and his eldest son were usually designated as the three lives.) Although the monks had been receiving occasional entry fines since the thirteenth century, the indentures themselves began mentioning fines only about 1520. These fines were still not high, usually two to four times the annual rent and in some cases, even less than the rent.[3]

1  Information for this paragraph comes from a variety of sources. See *ibid.*, pp.689, 692, 686; Finberg, *Tavistock Abbey*, p.130; Kerridge, 'The Movement of Rent', pp.19-23; Kew; 'The Land Market in Devon', pp.87-88, 210; Habakkuk, 'The Market for Monastic Property', pp.365, 370-71; Youings, 'Landlords in England', p.336.

2  DRO, L 1258, D 53 and D 73.

3  Finberg, *Tavistock Abbey*, pp.249-50; DRO, L 1258, D 53/31/5, D 53/31/6.

As the Dissolution approached, abbeys everywhere in England issued numerous long leases, an attempt to maximize revenue while the land remained under monastic control.[1] Needless to say, such indentures greatly limited the freedom of action of the new lay owners, and after 1539 Russell's agents did their best to convince tenants to renegotiate their terms. All leases contracted during 1538-39 were declared invalid by statute; in other instances, we can assume that Russell's agents used strong persuasion. Suddenly finding himself responsible for paying reserved rents to the crown and anxious to buy additional property, Russell found himself short of cash and welcomed receipt of new entry fines. An estate document indicates that at Hurdwick alone some nineteen new leases were issued in 1540, often to leaseholders already occupying the lands. The renegotiated leases did not increase annual rents but provided new fines and shortened the terms of tenure from three lives to two. They promised Russell £40.15s in additional income. No doubt the tenants would have been happier if left undisturbed in their holdings. Yet despite the new leases, Russell seems neither to have unduly antagonized his tenants nor inflicted hardship on them.[2]

Twenty-six leases from Hurdwick have been examined for the years 1540-55.[3] They exhibit continuity comparable to that revealed in the earlier monastic sample. Families whose names appeared in the fifteenth century renewed their leases under both Russell and his son Francis. At these renewals, while annual rents tended to remain constant, fines increased but often not greatly. Sometimes fine figures do not reveal the entire story. In 1522 Robert Wenton paid a fine of £1.13s.4d. and an annual rent of £2. In 1554, Thomas Wenton's fine was £2.13s.4d., his rent still £2. And Thomas leased a close more of land than Robert. Yet the increase in Thomas's fine was greater than first appears: Robert's lease had run for three lives while that of Thomas lasted only one life.[4]

Of the twenty-six Hurdwick leases negotiated during the period 1540-55, fourteen ran for two lives, seven for three lives (or a number of years determinable on three lives), two for one life. The fines show no consistent relationship with either the length of tenure or the annual rent payment. Whether the leases specifiy two or three lives, the fines

---

D 73/29/2 represents an unusually high fine.

1  Youings, 'Landlords in England', p. 227. see e.g., DRO, L 1258, D 53/12/1, D 53/24/6, D 53/27/7, D 53/31/7, D 53/32/3, D 53/40/3.

2  DRO, W 1258, D 49/2; Finberg, *Tavistock Abbey*, pp.270-71.

3  In the collection DRO, L 1258, 2/.

4  DRO, L 1258, D 53/31/6 and L 1258, 2/68-75.

average slightly more than four times the annual rent payments. In fact, contrary to all logic, the fines run slightly higher for the shorter tenures (see Table II). Studies of crown lands suggest that only in the 1560s did a clear relationship emerge between fines and rents. By then fine payments to the crown reflected the increased or improved annual value of the land in excess to the rent charged. But earlier crown leases did not embody this formula, and Russell's property reveals some of the same inconsistencies exhibited in crown leases during the 1540s[1] In one case at Hurdwick in 1544, the fine was actually less than the rent and in another instance in 1548, the rent and fine were equal; sometimes the indentures make no mention of fines at all[2] Nevertheless on other occasions, perhaps when annual value had increased more dramatically, the fines rose to the vicinity of six, seven, and once even fourteen times the value of the rent, here celarly departing from the custom of the manor and contemporary practices on crown lands[3]

### TABLE II: ENTRY FINES AS RENT MULTIPLES, 1539-1555

| Manor | Tenure | Total Fines | Total Rents | Multiple |
|---|---|---|---|---|
| Hurdwick | 2 lives | £51.14s.8d. | £11.17s.4d. | 4.35[a] |
| Hurdwick | 3 lives | £62.6s.8d. | £14.16s.8d. | 4.18[b] |
| Werrington | 2 lives | £178.5s.8d. | £41.19s. | 4.25[c] |
| Werrington | 3 lives | £83.1s. | £5.14s.1d. | 9.41[d] |

(a) ten leases; leases 2/5, 2/54, and two in 2/90 omitted because of insufficient information. (b) Eight leases; 2/98 and 2/117c illegible. (c) Forty-six leases; leases in 15/23c, 15/23k and 16/6 omitted; 15/23k is atypical (fine £42., rent £1.5s.6d.). When it is included, multiple rises to 5.1. (d) Seven leases; 15/23a is omitted because fine is very atypical (fine £45., rent £1.13s.4d.). When lease is included, multiple rises to 13.68.

At Werrington manor, Russell's agents negotiated fifty-nine leases during the years of his ownership. Eight ran for three lives, forty-eight for two lives, two for one life. Here fines were significantly greater the longer the tenure: 9.41 times the rent for three lives, as opposed to

1 For crown leases, see Habakkuk, 'The Market for Monastic Property', pp.370-71; also Kerridge, 'The Movements of Rent', p. 19.

2 DRO, L 1258, 2/49, 2/54, 2/32a, 2/98, 2/117c.

3 See DRO, L 1258, 2/46, 2/34, 2/42.

4.25 times the rent for two lives (see Table II). Probably the work of an agent, the discrepancy in rates explains why the shorter tenure so predominated at Werrington. As at Hurdwick, several indentures demonstrated both increased fines and continuity among tenants. For example, Richard Werying leased a furlong and a tenement in the parish of North Petherin for an annual rent of 7s. and an entry fine of £1.6s.8d. in 1541. When Joan Werying renewed the lease in 1554, she kept the same tenure and rent but paid a fine of £5., over fourteen times her annual rent payment.[1] In another, admittedly unusual example, the fine actually decreased. John Whenacot, also of North Petherin, agreed in 1543 to pay a fine of £4.19s. and an annual rent of 14s.7d. on two furlongs of land for a tenure of two lives. The lease was renegotiated in 1547; all the terms remained intact but the fine was lowered to £2. Apparently an additional payment in hand was motivation for the downward adjustment.[2] Other leases, negotiated during the 1550s and running either two or three lives, imposed fines from four to twenty-one times the value of rents.[3] The indentures at Werrington, like the ones at Hurdwick, show few increases that are exact multiples between rents and premium fine payments.

Russell's most eminent tenant was probably Dorothy, Lady Mountjoy who, as already noted, leased the house, gardens, parks, orchards, woods and meadows of Tavistock Abbey. Her indenture of 1541 stipulated a rent of £20 for sixty years, determinable on her death, and in addition she agreed to pay 13d. per bushel for receipt of rents in wheat from Plymstock, one of Russell's manors. When in 1553 her son, John Blount, rented the abbey for twenty-one years, he paid an entry fine of £100 , a new term reflecting inflationary pressures. Yet his annual rent remained £20 , and he continued to pay 13d. per bushel of Plymstock wheat.[4]

The Mountjoy lease reminds us that Russell was very much an absent landlord to all his western tenants. While he played the role of busy, distant lord privy seal, local men of gentry standing administered his western holdings. Many of the decisions attributed to him in reality mirror the influence and judgement of these local agents; hence some disparity between fines at Hurdwick and Werrington. Yet we can

1 DRO, L 1258, 15/18-20.

2 DRO, L 1258, 15/1. For another unusual example, see Dox lease in 1545 (17/9) where fine was lower than rent.

3 See e.g., DRO, L 1258, 17/10, 16/1, 15/9. 15/23a represents the highest fine (£45, on annual rent of £1.13s.4d.) but was very atypical.

4 See above, p. 105, n.4.

assume that Russell agreed with the basic thrust of the leases being negotiated in his name. William Larder had long been a trusted servant before Russell appointed him in 1541 as bailiff responsible for collecting revenues at Werrington manor. The chief steward for all the western lands, Hugh Trevanion, became a family friend who witnessed Russell's will.[1] Had Russell been dissatisfied with the performance of these men, he could have replaced them.

Russell belonged to a large group of Tudor landlords who had benefited from the distribution of monastic lands and was distinguished from the others only in that the bulk of his property came so exclusively from former monastic houses. Yet the economic behaviour of these new Tudor landlords defies pat generalizations. Some like Sir Ralph Sadler have been studied and their land management labelled 'shrewdly capitalistic'. Others like Sir William Petre are classified as moderates who refrained from extracting all possible income from their tenants.[2] Russell's rental policies place him in the second category.

The first Earl of Bedford did not participate in rack-renting and cannot be accused of exploiting his tenants. In the late 1550s and early 1560s, the Earl of Pembroke extracted fines on his estates that averaged thirty-six times the yearly rent.[3] In contrast those that Russell collected at Werrington in the early 1550s averaged approximately eleven times the yearly rent.[4] Russell's official responsibilities in the west, especially his concern for social stability after 1549, made him sensitive to complaints about rack-renting and to the political repercussions of such complaints. In the wake of the Western Uprising, he instructed the gentry to investigate Cornish landowners charged with oppressing and impoverishing their tenants. He spoke of 'pore men . . . grieved with uniust exactions by their land lordes . . .'. Although he attributed the abuses to 'the meaner sorte of gentylmen their servantes and others yet the infamye reddamdyth and not without some deserf unto others whyche be of most worshipfulls'. Ordering 'reformacion' and redress, he appears very much a foe to exploitative practices.[5]

But if Russell was not a ruthless, rack-renting capitalist was he a

1 DRO, W 1258, GE 1/10/3; Thomson, *Two Centuries of Family History*, pp.176-77.

2 Slavin, *Politics and Profits*, p.207; F.G. Emmison, *Tudor Secretary: Sir William Petre at Court and Home* (Cambridge, Mass., 1961), p. 269. See also Russell, *The Crisis of Parliaments*, p.118.

3 Kew, 'The Land Market in Devon', p.208.

4 DRO, L 1258, 15/7, 15/9, 15/12+14, 15/18-20, 15/23a, 15/23g, 12/23k (2 leases).

5 See above, p. 77, n. 2.

benevolent one interested in estate improvement and maximization of assets? The weight of the evidence suggests neither category is applicable and instead reveals him simply as a new owner trying to compensate for the inflated value of land. Tavistock rental income needed such adjustment by 1540.[1] We must add that neither Russell nor his agents were particularly mercenary, scientific, or even terribly consistent in pursuing their goals. Fine increases were much too illogical to be considered a systematic attempt at profit-making. Existing tenants were not deterred from making new and enlarged holdings. In fact, even with the increases, rental receipts probably did not keep pace with rising values although to answer this question we must know undertenancies, yields, tenant profit, and the rate of fine payments. We do know that as late as 1585, annual income at Werrington reached £128., a mere increment of £3. over the value of the manor in 1539. And fines had done no more than double the income since 1565.[2]

The quality of Devon's agriculture duly impressed contemporaries, and historians also rate it high.[3] Yet efficiency did not mean that the county's agriculture was commercialized in the capitalist sense. Devon remained too self-sufficient and remote for such a phenomenon.[4] Russell's behaviour was appropriate in such a context. His rental policies classify him as a sixteenth-century transitional figure. He can be identified neither as a paternal feudal lord, who saw his tenants as the source of military power, nor as a new type of landlord engaged in rationalized, profit-making ventures. Property brought with it status and influence, and herein lay its importance for Russell. Extensive acquisitions and higher entry fines were not enough to make him a capitalist.

Like other members of the nobility, Russell engaged in economic diversification and, in contrast to his rental policies, he invested capital for profit in mercantile and industrial ventures. Even in the 1520s while he was still a minor figure at court, he received commercial grants, including import and export licences.[5] Moreover, in 1528, his

1   Habakkuk, 'The Market for Monastic Property', p.364.

2   Youings, 'Landlords in England', p.346.

3   BL, Harl, MS. 5827, fol. 7. Finberg notes that the wheat yield at Hurdwick and Werrington was greater than at comparable manors in other counties. See Finberg, *Tavistock Abbey*, pp.113, 88, 91-92.

4   Joan Thirsk, 'The Farming Regions of England', *Agrarian History of England and Wales*, IV, 15.

5   *L.P.*, III(ii), 2074(5); IV(ii), 4231. Russell may have sold licences for profit but retained rights to the customs and tolls at Poole; PRO, E 315/418.

name appeared on a list of Cornish mine-owners,[1] and this interest in mining surfaced again in 1550 in a project to extract iron ore from Exmoor Forest. Russell and four colleagues from the west agreed to pay 6s.8d. per ton of ore to the crown and in return received all rights to the ore, including the right to erect mills for smelting.[2]

Russell also invested in shipping enterprises, a fact which may explain his strong defence of English trade rights in his official position as Privy Councillor. When the French inflicted damage on his property during war in 1543, the crown authorized Russell to capture as many French ships as possible.[3] Two years later he was involved at least financially in piracy against the Spanish. No longer themselves at war, Spaniards carried French goods only to meet harrassment and plunder at the hands of English captains, especially captains from the west country. One of their nemeses, Thomas Wyndham, seved as captain on a ship owned by Russell. In 1545 Wyndham captured the *Santa Maria de Guadalupe* with a cargo of French woad and wine. After all the spoils had been divided, Wyndham and Russell received £78. apiece from a prize worth £500. Protests from the Imperial ambassador, however, convinced the admiralty court and eventually the Privy Council itself to rule in favour of Spanish claims. In the end both Russell and Wyndham paid £85.9s.5d. as their share of the damages.[4] Yet this incident did not deter Russell from underwriting other such ventures, and in 1549 one of his own vessels was the victim of piracy attacks.[5]

In addition to pirateering, Wyndham and Russell showed interest in the exploration of new trade routes. Others shared the same concern. The desire to open new avenues of trade, especially the possibility of discovering a north-east passage, led in 1553 to the creation of the Russia or Muscovy Company. Over two hundred members, including seven peers, subscribed £25 each and thereby financed three ships, one of which eventually reached Russia. As a shareholder in this stock company, itself a new financial device, Russell invested captial but

---

1 *L.P.*, Addenda (i), 622.

2 *Cal. Pat. Rolls, Edw. VI*, III, 344-45 and Strype, *Ecclesiastical Memorials*, II(i), 431-32.

3 *L.P.*, XVIII(i), 474(21).

4 *APC*, I, 158, 265, 415, 435, 486; *Cal. S.P. Spain*, VIII, 198. Gordon Connell-Smith, *Forerunners of Drake* (London, 1954), pp.134-35, 181-82. Russell also had a fifty-ton vessel that joined the royal fleet: *L.P.*, XX(ii), 26.

5 *Cal. S.P. Spain*, IX, 338.

neither managed company affairs nor participated in actual trade. He died before receiving return on his investment.[1]

It is not possible to calculate the true extent of Bedford's fortune. In addition to his mercantile and landed income, he received fees, annuities, and gratuities associated with his service to the crown, many of which remained hidden. We know that Russell's most lucrative office was the keepership of the privy seal at an annual salary of £365, but we know nothing of the sealing fees he probably shared with his four clerks. His stipulated salary as lord warden and steward of the duchy of Cornwall (£20 and 50 marks respectively) took no account of gratuities.[2] The royal parks and forests under his charge carried specified fees but profits from herbage and pannage are rarely cited.[3] Even when income is known, it is sometimes difficult to weigh in real terms. For instance, Russell was paid £1,000. per year when he served actively as lord president of the Council of the West, but the sum did no more than cover expenses.[4] Altogether Russell's fees even with his rental income did not always cover costs and keep him solvent.

Some figures are available which allow us to compare Russell's wealth and status with that of friends and colleagues at court. The normal income for a noble in 1539 lay between £600 and £1,500 Russell's landed income after Tavistock put him securely in his peer group. A few years later his assets were assessed for the subsidy of 1545 at £1,626, a sum which supposedly included lands, free rents, services, property held by wardship, annuities, and fees. The sum was reasonably accurate since assessment figures were not grossly distorted during the reign of Henry VIII. Average income for all forty-four nobles at the time of the subsidy was £873; hence Russell clearly enjoyed wealth far above the norm. As Henry's reign drew towards its close, he stood with some fourteen peers whose income exceeded £1,000. although he was still worth much less than the Duke of Norfolk, the wealthiest peer in 1545 with an annual income of £3,333.6s.8d.[5]

1   *Cal. Pat. Rolls, Mary,* II, 55-59 and Strype, *Ecclesiastical Memorials,* III(i), 520-21; T.S. Willan., *The Muscovy Merchants of 1555* (Manchester, 1953), pp. 6-7. 10-11.

2   *L.P.,* XVII, 1251(7); XIV(i), 1354(12).

3   When Restmorel and Boconnoc were 'disparked', Russell was awarded an annuity of £17. by the court of general serveyors; PRO, E 315/106, fol. 18. By 1550 he also received an additional annuity of £23.6s.8d.; Richardson, *The Report of the Royal Commission of 1552,* p.133.

4   Thomson, *Two Centuries of Family History,* pp.172-73.

5   Miller, 'The Tudor Peerage', p.129; 'Subsidy Assessments of the Peerage in the Sixteenth Century', pp.18-19, 21, 27-29.

During the reign of Edward, Russell added approximately £670 to his annual income through free grants. Only one inquisition post mortem survives and no comprehensive figure exists for Bedford's income at his death, but as already noted, by 1558 the family's lands brought over £2,000 in annual rental receipts. The second earl, in a group whose gross rentals ranged from £2,000 to £2,999, was among the twenty-three greatest magnates in the realm. The Herberts, one of the other new noble families, now surpassed the Bedfords, but included within the same category were the families of Browne, Paget, Rich, Seymour, and Wriothesley, all colleagues who had served with John Russell at the court of Henry VIII.[1]

The end result represents a staggering financial achievement on Russell's part. His political and landed careers had worked together, reinforcing each other. Impressive wealth began because he pleased the king and remained intact because he always respected political realities. But Russell did not rest content with the royal initiative; in the 1540s especially, he undertook substantial purchases and leaseholds in order to expand his property. When his economic activities are viewed in total, he can seem financially shrewd — diversifying his investments to include mercantile as well as landed interests, employing multiple methods of acquisition, willing to forego temporary cash surpluses for long-term gains. Yet he remained a sixteenth-century Henrician, not always respecting the logic of economic gain, thinking in terms of status rather than fluid assets, combining loyalty and influence in such a way as to found a great family fortune based on land.

---

1 Stone, *The Crisis of the Aristocracy*, Appendix VIII, p.760.

# IN RETROSPECT

Any assessment of Russell must pay tribute to his political shrewdness. Not only Russell but all the Henricians who survived the political and religious vicissitudes at court are naturally and legitimately called *politiques*, pragmatists, and opportunists. Contemporaries perceived the situation clearly enough and minced no words in explaining political realities. William Paulet, Marquis of Winchester, whose career so closely parallelled Russell's, realistically described himself as 'sprung from willow, not the oak'.[1] Sir John Mason, a diplomatic envoy who served with Russell, advised colleagues to speak little and write less, to pursue moderate policies so that they might ingratiate themselves with all parties and factions.[2] More removed from the source of power, Bishop John Ponet witnessed the despoliation of church lands and ultimately became a Marian exile. He presents the most derogatory testimony, indicting councillors of the prince for their ruthlessness and deceit; 'a man maie not trust no belieue them, either by their wordes, othes, or hande writings further than he seeth and heareth them, and scarcely so farre'. Russell shared Paulet's flexibility and achieved a comparable degree of success at court. His career also reflects the moderation counselled by Mason. But in Russell's case at least pragmatism did not create the Machiavellianism which Ponet denounced.

Simple, unglamorous qualities accounted for Russell's political good fortune. Much of his progress he owed simply to hard work. His reputation for industry and conscientiousness survived even into the late Elizabethan period.[4] He performed competently for the king for thirty years before receiving a title and then served diligently for sixteen additional years. Another factor crucial to his success: loyalty and prudence dominated his ambition. Russell indulged in legitimate aspirations that could be satisfied within the system. He refrained from grasping after the highest power but instead nurtured his relationship with Henry VIII, whom he understood. The patronage and favours he bestowed reflect no pattern outside the western interest and show no

1  See Emmison, *Tudor Secretary*, p.295.

2  Smith, *Henry VIII*, p.242.

3  Ponet, 'A Short Treatise of Politike Power', p.139.

4  See Thomas Nashe, *The Vnfortvnate Traueller* (1594) in *The Works of Thomas Nashe*, ed, Ronald B. McKerrow (Oxford, 1958), II, 264. The incident that Nashe describes cannot be substantiated but is indicative of Russell's favourable posthumous standing. I am grateful to Dr. Daniel Traister for the reference.

attempt to build a following or a party of his own. During Edward's reign, once the hand of a strong monarch was removed, faction became inescapable, and true to his pragmatism, Russell bowed to prevailing political influences. But too prudent and restrained to become one of the worst of the schemers, he served as henchman neither to Somerset nor Northumberland.

His character contained contradictory impulses. On the most dangerous matters, he shrewdly kept his own counsel; most noticeably, he did not advocate that the crown pursue any one religious policy. But pragmatism notwithstanding, he was no time-server, and like others of his colleagues, he spoke with surprising frankness on occasion. Figures at court including Anne Boleyn, the Duke of Norfolk, Henry VIII himself, and later the Duke of Somerset heard Russell voice unpopular opinions. He defended Wolsey in 1530, criticized the Boulogne campaign in 1544, and argued with the lord protector in 1549. He spoke his mind on those issues which moved or angered him provided that he felt politically secure. Still there were no guarantees at the Tudor court. Russell weighed and minimized his political risks, but he could not eliminate them altogether before speaking out.

Among contemporaries he enjoyed a reputation for honesty and integrity. An impressive tribute to his character came from the pen of Sir Thomas Wyatt, the poet-courtier who had accompanied Russell to Rome in 1527 and remained his friend thereafter. In 1537 Wyatt's son was recently wed, and the father wrote letters of advice to the fifteen-year-old bridgegroom, among them the prescription:

> Think and ymagine alwais that, you are in presens of some honist man that you know, as Sir Jhon Russel, your father-in-law, your vnkle, parson, or some other such, and ye shal, if at ony time ye find a plesur in naughtye touchis, remember what shame it were afore thes men to doo naughtily.[1]

Wyatt repeated his exhortations in a subsequent letter and expressed the fear that his son might mistake the appearance of integrity for the reality. The quality that Wyatt had in mind 'is no comen thing . . . but so mitch it si the more goodbye for that it is so rare and strong'[2]; with this definition for him to have cited Russell as a model of behaviour was serious praise indeed.

Russell possessed several traits that made him likeable: amiability,

---

[1]  Kenneth Muir, *The Life and Letters of Sir Thomas Wyatt* (Liverpool, 1963), p.39 and *L.P.*, XII(i), 1299.

[2]  Muir, *Life and Letters of Wyatt*, p.42.

congeniality, and even compassion. His associates in the west as well as his colleagues at court have left behind only kindly references. Quarrels, such as those with Edward Seymour, were the exception, not the rule. How some colleagues regarded and respected him is evident from the enthusiastic testimony of John Williams, master of the jewel-house, who served with Russell and Sir Francis Bryan in the Pilgrimage of Grace: 'God never died for a better couple'.[1] His sense of compassion appears in various incidents: his solicitude for Wolsey in 1530, his concern about unpaid labourers in the west in 1545, his actions for the poor as lord lieutenant after the Western Uprising. Naturally enough, from his point of view, he used extreme severity when dealing with rebels and traitors. And even his compassion reflects his ever-present pragmatism: a content peasantry provided the best guarantee for stability.

More than politics claimed his attention. We know him as an intelligent man, fluent in languages. He had contacts with English humanist circles in Italy, probably first cultivated during his travels abroad in the 1520s. He seems also to have been interested in the drama. As lord admiral, he had a company of players whom he sent to Plymouth to perform in 1540.[2] But it is safe to assume that outside his official responsibilities, Russell devoted most of his time and attention to his family and property. Those references to the family that survive suggest he enjoyed a compatible marriage and found a valuable help-mate in his wife Anne, who like her husband served at court. Blessed with only one child, Russell naturally groomed his son to follow in his footsteps.[3]

Despite his dramatic personal success, in many ways the first earl was not an outstanding figure. Whether due to his prudence or his 'limited vision',[4] Russell's name can be associated with no single line of state policy, no important piece of legislation, no permanent institutional legacy. He may well have influenced political decisions but, if so, his was that subtle, unobtrusive influence most difficult to detect. Only once in 1549 did the political consequences of his actions clearly emerge. Nevertheless, his very lack of distinction makes him typical of a generation of courtiers who supported the Tudors in order to become the new men at court. Like so many of his colleagues —

---

1 *L.P.*, XI, 888.

2 Cecily Radford, 'Three Centuries of Playgoing in Exeter', *Transactions of the Devonshire Assocation* 82 (1952), 245.

3 See Thomson, *Two Centuries of Family History*, p.86.

4 See Beer's description in *Northumberland*, p.125.

Paulet, Browne, Herbert — Russell began his career in the king's household. Versatility characterized his responsibilities. As servants to the crown, he and his contemporaries exchanged the roles of courtier, councillor, diplomat and soldier as the situation at hand demanded. Service not policy was to be their contribution.

Viewed from the perspective of Russell's career, government in the sixteenth century remained strongly personal in nature. From the household he moved into offices associated with public government, from gentleman usher eventually to lord privy seal. Many of these offices were important not just for the duties they entailed but also for the opportunities and contacts which accompanied them. Influence and connection still underlay the everyday work of government. Although significant administrative innovations date from Henry's reign, from Russell's point of view they hardly represented the essence of government.

He made a valuable, personal contribution to the governance of the western counties. The crown briefly attempted an institutional, bureaucratic approach there, but the Council of the West did not survive. Instead the west was integrated more tightly into the realm through Russell's authority as the foremost aristocrat in the area, that is, through informal influence, patronage, and special commissions. If, on the one hand, his experiences in the 1540s revealed the limitations of this personal approach, on the other hand, he attained a good degree of success as lord lieutenant in the 1550s.

Personal monarchy in England demanded the allegiance of its aristocracy if political stability were to be retained. Russell recognized this basic political reality and thus supported strong monarchy and an undisputed succession. As a consequence, he and his like provided a positive stabilizing force for a still precarious nation state. Rewards and self-interest reinforced his Erastian principles, but they should not detract from what his former biographer rightly describes as his 'passionate loyalty to the crown'.[1] Loyalty was his greatest service to the dynasty.

[1] Thomson, *Two Centuries of Family History*, p.198.   Cf. Emmison's description of Petre in *Tudor Secretary*, p.296.

# MANUSCRIPT SOURCES

Bedford County Record Office, Bedford: Russell Estate Papers: Boxes 262, 277, 299, 300

Bedford Office, London: Papers of the First Earl, Volumes 3, 5, 5A

Bodleian Library, Oxford: Ashmolean Manuscripts

British Library: Additional, Cotton, Harleian, Lansdowne, Royal, and Sloane Manuscripts

Devon County Record Office, Exeter: Russell Estate Papers: W 1258, L 1258

History of Parliament Trust, London

Inner Temple Library, London: The Petyt Collection 538

Public Record Office: Chancery (C 1); Duchy of Lancaster (DL 3); Lord Chamberlain's Accounts (LC 2); Exchequer (E 36, 308, 310, 315, 318, 326); Feet of Fines [CP 25(2)]; Privy Council (PC 2); Privy Seal Office (PSO 2); Court of Requests (Req. 2); Special Collections, Ministers' and Receivers' Accounts (SC 6); Court of Star Chamber (Sta. Cha. 2); State Papers, Henry VIII (S.P. 1, 2, 3); State Papers, Domestic, Edward VI (S.P. 10) and Mary (S.P. 11); State Papers, Foreign, Edward VI (S.P. 68) and Mary (S.P. 69); Court of Wards (Wards 8, 9); Court of Admiralty (HCA); Prerogative Court of Canterbury, Wills.

Widener Library, Cambridge, Massachusetts: Exeter City Muniments; Microfilm Collection

Woodruff Library, Atlanta, Georgia: Seymour Papers at Longleat House, Wiltshire: Manuscripts of the Marquis of Bath; Microfilm Collection

# INDEX

Acton, manor of, 107
Amersham, manor of, 14, 103n
Andover, 84
Antwerp, 10, 89
Arundel, Earl of, *see* Fitz Alan, Henry
Arundell, Sir Thomas, 39, 41, 83, 87
Aske, Robert, 27-8
Aston Abbots, manor of, 106, 116
Awliscombe, rectory of, 105

Barbaunce, Martin, 80n
Barnard Castle, 26
Barnstaple, 40
Basset, John, 36
Bath, Earl of, *see* Bourchier, John
Bedford, Earls of, *see* Russell
Bedford House, Exeter, 68n, 105
Bellerica (Somerset), 114n
Berry, John, 73n
Berwick, John, 53
Berwick, manor of, 2, 4, 14, 102
Bishop's Clyst, manor of, 109, 111-2
Bishop's Tawton, manor of, 109, 111-2
Blackawton, manor and rectory of, 105
Blagge, Sir George, 51n
Blintfield, manor of, 2, 102
Blount, Dorothy, Lady Mountjoy, 105, 121
Blount, John, 121
Blount William, Lord Mountjoy, 6
Boconnoc, park of, 109-10, 113n, 125n
Bodmin, 70
Boleyn, Anne, Queen of England, 16n, 21-3, 25, 128
Bonner, Edmund, Bishop of London, 34, 42, 46
Boulogne, 6, 47-8, 50, 59, 87, 88, 128
Bourchier, John, Earl of Bath, 62n, 69
Boyton (Cornwall), 114n
Brandon, Charles, Duke of Suffolk, 26-7, 46-9, 67
Broughton, John, 15
Browne, Sir Anthony: service at court, 4, 16-7, 48, 51, 130; knighthood, 8; Pilgrimage of Grace, 26; actions during protectorate, 55, 57; relationship with Russell, 17, 42n, 47; estates, 126; religious views, 42

Bryan, Sir Francis, 8, 8n, 26-7, 113, 129
Buckingham, Duke of, *see* Stafford, Edward
Burrington, manor of, 105
Bury, monastery of, 106
Buse, Jeffrey, 79
Buse, John, 79

Calais, 5-7, 24, 45, 89
Camelton (Bedfordshire), 114n
Carew, Sir Nicholas, 8n, 16
Carew, Sir Peter, 40-1, 70, 73, 81
Caryfytzpan, manor of, 105
Casale, Gregory, 18-9
Castillon, Gaspard de Coligny, French ambassador, 31
Catherine of Aragon, Queen of England, 18, 20, 23n
Catherine of York, 64
Cavell, Sir Humphrey, 40
Cavell, William, 40n
Chaldon Herring, manor of, 102
Chambers, John, abbot of Peterborough, 37, 42
Chapuys, Eustace, Imperial ambassador, 46
Charles V, Emperor: alliance with England, 1523-25, 9-10, 12, 17-8;
    campaigns of 1527, 19-20; alliance with England, 1543-44, 46-8;
    possible mediator, 48-9; policies during reign of Edward VI, 87,
    89, 94; Mary's marriage, 96, 98
Charles, Duke of Bourbon and Constable of France, 9-12, 13, 18-9,
    20, 47
Charles, Duke of Savoy, 11
Chenies, manor of, 14, 45n, 100, 102-3, 104n, 105, 106, 108, 116
Cheyney, John, 103
Cheyney, Sir Thomas, 16n, 16-7, 23n, 31, 78, 93-5
Christow, manor of, 105
Chumleigh, manor of, 113n
Cinque Ports, warden of, *see* Cheyney, Thomas
Clement VII, Pope, 12, 18-20
Clerk, John, Bishop of Bath and Wells, 11
Clerk, Roger, 108n
Clinton, Edward, Lord, 78, 97
Clopton Hall, manor of, 106, 116
Clyst Heath, battle of, 71
Clyst Honiton, manor of, 112
Clyst St. Mary, 70
Coldhall (Suffolk), 107
Common Prayer, Book of, 70, 76, 83

Cornwall, duchy of, 30, 39-40, 64, 65, 125
Cornwood, manor of, 105
Council of the North, 66
Council of Wales, 109
Council of the West: jurisdiction and purpose, 30-1, 65-6, 76-7, 79;
    membership, 39, 65n, 67, 68, 73, 115; Russell as lord president,
    30, 65-6, 77, 79, 81, 106, 125; demise, 66, 69, 74; subsequent
    influence, 76-7, 79, 81
Court of augmentations, 101, 107, 108
Courtenay, Edward, Earl of Devonshire, 96
Courtenay family, 63, 67, 68, 75, 96
Courtenay, Henry, Earl of Devonshire and Marquis of Exeter:
    position at court, 17, 25, 64; position in the west, 62-4, 105, 111;
    estates, 39, 64n, 105; attainder and execution, 31, 64
Courtenay, Lord William, 63-4
Covent Garden, 113
Coverdale, Miles, 42, 79n
Covington, manor of, 14
Cowick, manor of, 105
Cranmer, Thomas, Archbishop of Canterbury, 32-3, 34-5, 41, 51,
    55, 57, 82, 86
Credition Park, 111
Cromwell, Richard, 26, 48
Cromwell, Thomas, Earl of Essex, 21, 22, 27, 37, 44, 51, 68;
    reorganization of Privy Council, 29; lord privy seal, 50-1; re-
    organization of Council of the North, 66; creation of Council of
    the West, 65, 76; relationship with Russell, 23, 25, 28, 34-5, 41;
    fall from power, 34-5, 44, 66
Crouche, servant to Edward Seymour, 52-4
Croy, Adrian de, Count of Roeulx (Rue), 48
Culpepper, Sir Thomas, 45n

Darcy, Thomas, Lord, 24, 27, 32, 42
Darcy, Sir Thomas, 111
Delft, Francois van der, Imperial ambassador, 56n, 57, 58, 87, 89,
    91, 94
Denbury, manor of, 105
Denny, Sir Anthony, 57, 57n
Denny, Thomas, 17
Denys family, 73
Denys, Sir Thomas, 69, 111
Derby, Earl of, see Stanley, Henry
Dereham, Francis, 45n
Doncaster, 26-7

Dorchester, 1-2, 102
Dorset, Marquis of, *see* Grey, Henry
Dover, 90n
Downing, Edmund, 114n
Dudley, John, Viscount Lisle, Earl of Warwick and Duke of Northumberland, 61, 97, 99n; service under Henry VIII, 4, 33, 51, 56n; Henry VIII's will, 55; during protectorate, 56-8; *coup* of 1549, 82, 84; consolidation of power, 86-7, 88n, 94, 112; as head of government, 78, 81, 88-92, 113; relationship with Russell, 52, 86-7, 91-5, 128; estates, 113; Device of 1553, 92-5
Dunheved, 40-1
Dunkeswell Abbey, 105-6, 107
Durham, 26

Edgcumbe family, 39n, 41, 67, 73
Edgcumbe, Sir Piers, 39n
Edgcumbe, Sir Richard, 69
Edward IV, King of England, 64
Edward VI, King of England, 54, 60, 88, 89n, 96; accession, 55; coronation, 56, 57; Council, 44, 54-9, 69-71, 74, 76, 77n, 78-95; *coup* of 1549, 83, 85; alienation of crown and episcopal lands, 84, 92, 109, 111-4, 126; royal finances, 90; progress of 1552, 80; Device of 1553, 92, 95; death, 86, 92-3
Elizabeth, Princess, 59-60
Eltham Ordinances, 13, 16-7, 31n
Enclosures, 70, 77, 82, 114
Enfield House, 55
Essex, Earl of, *see* Cromwell, Thomas and Parr, William
Exe Island, 74
Exeter, city of, 39, 68n, 77, 80, 105, 106; relations with Russell, 68-9, 74-5, 80n, 81, 98; under siege, 71, 73-4, 85n
Exeter, Marquis of, *see* Courtenay, Henry
Exmoor Forest, 105n, 124
Eybury (Northamptonshire), 107

Feckenham, John, abbot of Westminster, 42
Fenny Bridges, battle of, 71
Field of Cloth of Gold, 8
Finneshade (Northamptonshire), 107
Fitz Alan, Henry, Earl of Arundel, 83, 87, 93-5, 96, 98
Fitzroy, Henry, Duke of Richmond, 20
Fitzwalter, Lord, *see* Radcliffe, Thomas
Fitzwilliam, William, Earl of Southampton, 26-7, 45, 46
Fitzwilliam, William (Russell's kinsman), 36-7, 41

Flanders, 89
Forde Mansion (Devon), 110
Foxe, John, 25n, 41
France: negotiations with, 48, 50, 58, 75, 88-9; war in 1513, 6; war 1522 ff., 8-10, 12; war scare of 1539, 64; war 1544 ff., 46-50, 67-8, 70; war in 1549, 84; *see also* Francis I
Francis I, King of France, 7n, 9, 12, 20, 58
Frockmer, Elisabeth, 3n
Fryer Pyes (Middlesex), 107
Fuller, Thomas, 3, 104

Gage, Sir John, 58
Gale, John, 36, 40, 41
Gardiner, Stephen, Bishop of Winchester, 32, 42, 46, 49-50, 90n, 96, 97, 98
Gardiner, William, 40
Gascoigne, *see* Russell, Stephen and Henry
Geston (Lincoln), 107
Godolphin, Sir William, 39, 77
Goodrich, Thomas, Bishop of Ely, 87
Grenville family, 39n, 40
Grenville, Lady Maud, 40n, 67
Grenville, Sir Richard, 67, 69, 73
Grey Henry, Marquis of Dorset and Duke of Suffolk, 62n, 87
Grey, Lady Jane, 92-3, 113
Grey, William, Lord, 71, 92
Guildford, Sir Edward, 8n
Guildford, Sir Henry, 8n
Guisnes, 45
Guistinian, Sebastian, Venetian ambassador, 7

Hampton Court, 82
Hanford (Devon), 110
Hastings, Sir Edward, 93
Hastings, Francis, second Earl of Huntingdon, 92
Hastings, George, first Earl of Huntington, 26
Haverell, manor of, 104
Haydon, John, alias Heydon, 39, 106
Helston, 69
Heneage, Sir Thomas, 16, 21
Henry VII, King of England, 3-4, 5, 31n, 63, 100n
Henry VIII, King of England, 111, 128; changes in his household, 7-9, 16-7; divorce, 20, 21, 22; war and diplomacy, 9-10, 18-9, 45-

50, 67; new nobles, 30-1, 101, 126; attitude toward Russell, 4-10, 13-4, 17, 28, 30-3, 44, 51; patronage of Russell, 7, 14, 17, 24n, 30-1, 54, 56-7, 62, 64-5, 104-5, 112; visit to Chenies, 45n, 103; land exchanges with Russell, 107, 113n; his design for the west, 31, 62-5; old age, 33, 51, 51n-2n; will, 33, 54-5, 94; death, 55; grants of 1547, 56-7

Herbert, William, Earl of Huntingdon, 107

Herbert, William, Earl of Pembroke, 57, 78n, 88n, 92, 96, 99; courtier, 17, 57n, 130; Western Uprising of 1549, 71, 77n, 85n; *coup* of 1549, 82-6; accession crisis of 1553, 93-5; Wyatt's rebellion, 97; estates, 113, 122, 126

Herring, Elisabeth, 3n

Hersham, manor of, 104

Hertford, Earl of, *see* Seymour, Edward

Heylon, manor of, 104

Hinton St. George, 70

Hoby, Sir Philip, 86

Holbein, Hans, the Younger, 44

Honiton, 71

Horsey, Sir John, 68, 115

Hooker, John, *see* Vowell, John

Hopton (Hertfordshire), 114n

Hough (Lincoln), 107

Howard, Agnes, Duchess of Norfolk, 16n

Howard, Katherine, Queen of England, 15n, 45

Howard, Thomas, Earl of Surrey and Duke of Norfolk: Pilgrimage of Grace, 26-7; military compaigns of 1540s, 45-50, 67; intrigues of 1540s, 32, 42; relationship with Russell, 8, 48, 128; wealth, 125; attainder, 52n, 56

Hundred Years War, 2

Huntingdon, Earl of, *see* Hastings, Francis and George, and Herbert, William

Hurdwick, manor of, 105, 118-21, 123

Hussee, John, 36

Hussey, Sir John, 104

Ingliscombe, manor of, 107, 116

Ingliscombe, parsonage of, 108

Isenhamstead, see Chenies

James V, King of Scotland, 45

Jerningham, Sir Richard, 6, 7, 15, 30

Joanna, Queen Consort to Philip, Archduke of Austria and King of Castile, 3

Kayneston, manor of, 110
Kenninghall, 92
Ketyll, Thomas, 106
King's Langley, park of, 110
Kingston, Sir Anthony, 72
Kingston, Sir William, 7, 31
Kirby (Northamptonshire), 107
Knight, William, Bishop of Bath and Wells, 109n

La Pole, Richard, 7
La Tour, Alice de, 2, 3n
Lannoy, Charles de, viceroy of Naples, 12, 19
Lamewath, manor of, 104
Lancaster, 26
Larder, William, 122
Laverton, manor of, 107
League of Cognac, 18
Leland, John, 102
Lincoln, 26-7
Lisle, Lady Honor, 36, 40n
Lisle, Lord, see Plantagenet, Arthur
Lord lieutenancy: during Henry VIII's reign, 49, 67-8; during
    Edward VI's reign, 63, 70 ff., 76-9, 81, 92, 129, 130; during
    Mary's reign, 81
Ludgarshall (Wiltshire), 114n

Manners, Thomas, Earl of Rutland, 26
Margaret of Savoy, 10
Marillac, Charles de, French ambassador, 34-5
Mary I, Queen of England, 25, 40, 81; as Princess, 18, 65n; accession,
    82, 92-6; Council, 95-9; Wyatt's rebellion, 81, 97, 98; marriage,
    81, 96-9; attitude towards Anne and John Russell, 15, 94-5, 97,
    114
Mary Stuart, Queen of Scots, 88
Mason, Sir John, 88, 93-4, 127
Matte, Perceval de, 7
Medmenham, monastery of, 108
Montreuil, siege of, 47-8. 69
Moor Park, 23, 25
More, Sir Thomas, 8, 9-10, 13
Moreton, manor of, 102
Morleaux, battle of, 8
Mountjoy, Lord and Lady, see Blount
Muscovy Company, 89, 124-5

Naples, viceroy of, *see* Lannoy, Charles de
Neville, Sir Edward, 8n
Neville, Henry, Earl of Westmorland, 96
Newark, 26-7
Norfolk, Duchess of, *see* Howard, Agnes
Norfolk, Duke of, *see* Howard, Thomas
Norris, Sir Henry, 16
Northampton, Marquis of, *see* Parr, William
North Petherin (Devon), 121
Northumberland, Duke of, *see* Dudley, John
Nottingham, 26

Othorpe (Leicestershire), 107
Oundle, monastery of, 110, 113n
Oxford, Earl of, *see* Vere, John de

Pace, Richard, 10-3
Paget, William, Lord, 85; service during Henry VIII's reign, 4, 33, 50, 51; during the protectorate, 55-61, 88; *coup* of 1549, 82, 86; during Warwick's ascendancy, 87, 88-9, 92; fall from Council, 87; accession crisis of 1553, 93-4; Mary's Council, 95-8; Wyatt's rebellion, 97; relationship with Russell, 53-4, 115; estates, 111, 115, 126; religious views, 43
Parr, William, Earl of Essex and Marquis of Northampton, 26-7, 31, 56, 88n
Parva Crawford, (Dorset), 110
Paulet family, 70, 73
Paulet, Sir Hugh, 69, 77
Paulet, William, Lord St John, Earl of Wiltshire and Marquis of Winchester, 23n, 60, 99, 127; service at court, 4, 29, 51, 58n, 130; during protectorate, 56-7; during Warwick's ascendancy, 87, 92; accession crisis of 1553, 93, 95; honors and gifts from the crown, 31, 55-7, 87n, 113; relationship with Wolsey, 22; friendship with Russell, 34, 52, 87; religious views, 43
Pavia, battle of, 12, 18
Peachy, Sir John, 8n
Pedmore (Buckinghamshire), 107
Pembroke, Earl of, *see* Herbert William
Peryn, John, abbot of Tavistock, 38
Peterborough, 37
Petre, Sir William, 88, 93, 98, 122
Philibert, Emmanuel, Count of Piedmont, 75
Philip, Archduke of Austria and King of Castile, 3, 98
Philip II, King of Spain, 75, 95, 97n, 98-9

Piedmont, Prince of, *see* Philibert, Emmanuel
Pilgrimage of Grace, 25-8, 62, 64, 72, 129
Plantagenet, Arthur, Viscount Lisle, 23, 24, 36, 52
Plymouth, 70, 98-9, 129
Plymstock, manor of, 105, 121
Pointz, Francis, 8n
Pole, Reginald,, Cardinal, 24, 36, 64
Pollard family, 38, 67, 73
Pollard, Sir Hugh, 69
Pollard, Sir John, 38, 40
Pollard, Sir Lewis, 111
Pollard, Sir Richard, 110
Ponet, John, Bishop of Winchester, 127
Pontefract, 26
Poole, 69
Pope, *see* Clement VII
Portsmouth, 49, 69
Poynings, Sir Edward, 6
Privy chamber, 5, 13, 17, 21, 31, 60, 86
Privy Council: Russell's entry, 29; under Henry VIII, 33, 44-5, 49-50, 51n-2n, 64, 103, 124; Edward's Regency Council, 54-7; under the protectorate, 57-9; Western Uprising, 70-1, 73, 76, 77n, 84-5; relations with the city of Exeter, 68, 74-5, 81; *coup* of 1549, 82-3, 85-6; during Warwick's ascendancy, 78-81, 86-92; alienation of episcopal lands, 111-2; accession crisis of 1553, 92-5; under Queen Mary, 95-9
Privy seal office, 50-1, 125

Radcliffe, Henry, second Earl of Sussex, 93
Radcliffe, Thomas, Lord Fitzwalter, third Earl of Sussex, 98-9
Rebellions of 1549, 60-1, 69-74, 80, 82-5; *see also* Western Uprising
Reformation, 22, 25, 41, 109
Renard, Simon, Imperial ambassador, 42n, 50, 96
Restormel, park of, 109, 110, 125n
Rich, Richard, Lord, 43, 56, 87, 92-3, 126
Richmond, Duke of, *see* Fitzroy, Henry
Rochester, Sir Robert, 98
Rochford, Lady Jane, 15n
Rogers, Sir Edward, 41
Rome, 11-2, 18-20, 22, 128
Rosel, Hugo de, 1
Rowe, John, 67
Rue, Count of, *see* Croy, Adrian de
Russell, Alice, *see* La Tour, Alice de and Wyse, Alice

Russell, Anne, Lady Bedford, 31n, 38; service at court, 15, 94, 129; marriage to Russell, 14-6, 129; earlier marriages, 15, 103; children, 15-6; character, 16; estates and jointure, 14, 30n, 100, 102-3, 104n; funeral, 42

Russell, Edward, third Earl of Bedford, 1

Russell, Francis, second Earl of Bedford: birth, 15-6; offices and commissions, 37, 95, 111; father's attitudes and influence, 37, 95n, 97, 98, 99-100, 129; accession crisis of 1553, 95, 97; involvement in Wyatt's rebellion, 97, 98; position in the west, 31; parliamentary patronage, 40; estates, 99-100, 101, 102-3, 119, 126; religious views, 94

Russell, Henry (John's great-grandfather), 1-2, 3n

Russell, Henry (John's uncle), 2, 3n

Russell, James, 1-2, 3n, 4, 102

Russell, Joan (John's stepmother), 4, 102

Russell, John, first Earl of Bedford: family background, 1-2, 3n; early education, 2-3; linguistic abilities, 3, 17, 129; gentleman usher, 5, 130; military service at Calais, 5-7; diplomatic assignments, 9-12, 14, 17-21, 46, 58-9, 88-9; relationship with Wolsey, 5, 6-8, 13-4, 16-7, 18n, 21-2, 36, 128, 129; courtier (see also his offices), 4-5, 7-8, 16-7, 24-5, 60, 129-30; gentleman of the privy chamber, 13-7, 21, 31; knight marshal of the household, 9; wound at Morleaux, 8, 44; knighthood, 8, 20n; marriage, 14-6, 102, 129; sheriff for Dorset and Somerset, 23n, 65; membership in Lincoln's Inn, 39n, 41, 106; relationship with Cromwell, 23, 25, 28, 34-5, 41; friendship with Lord Lisle, 24, 36, 52; Pilgrimage of Grace, 25-8; Privy Councillor during Henry's reign, 28-9, 33-5, 44-6, 49-50, 51n-2n, 63, 68, 104, 106; comptroller, 29, 30n, 103; grants of 1539, 30, 62, 64-5, 104-5, 112; Knight of the Garter, 30; lord president of the Council of the West, 30, 65-7, 76-8, 81, 106, 125; lord admiral, 44, 45, 66, 106, 129; lord privy seal, 44, 45, 50-3, 58-60, 78-80, 91-4, 95n-6n, 98-9, 125, 130; ex officio president of the court of requests, 51, 79, 91; letter of marque against France, 1543, 124; captain of the vanguard, 1544, 44, 46-8; attitude toward war of 1544, 47-50, 128; high steward of Oxford University, 44n; lord lieutenant, 49, 63, 67-8, 70-9, 81, 129, 130; relationship with Henry VIII, 4-5, 7, 9-10, 13-4, 28, 31-3, 46-8, 51, 127, 130; Henry's will, 54; high steward for Edward VI's coronation, 57; Privy Councillor during Edward's reign, 43, 54-61, 78-9, 86-94; English trade claims, 58, 89, 124; attitude toward protectorate, 55-7; relationship with Edward Seymour, 43, 52-4, 83-5, 128, 129; fall of Thomas Seymour, 59-60; coup of 1549, 82-6, 129; relationship with Dudley, 52n, 86-7, 91-5, 112, 113, 128; earldom, 82, 84, 87; position during Somerset's trial 87-8;

accession crisis of 1553, 91-5; relationship with Mary, 94-5, 97; Privy Councillor during Mary's reign, 95-9, 114; mission to escourt Philip of Spain, 97-9; nature of his contribution, 31-2, 62-3, 76-81, 91, 127, 129-30; character, 4, 12, 24, 25, 32, 34, 60, 91, 95, 127-9; portraits, 43; attendance at Parliament, 23, 59n, 77n, 80n, 93, 93n-4n, 98n, 99; attitude toward the poor, 69, 76-7, 79-80, 122, 129; attitude toward Spain, 42n, 46, 58, 89, 96, 124; military strategist, 47-50, 72, 83-4, 84n-5n; official responsibilities in the west, 30-1, 38-41, 46, 49, 60-81, 83-4, 105, 122, 130; patronage, 29, 35-43, 51, 67, 74-5, 127-8, 130; wardships, 4, 38, 110; protecting and furthering son's career, 37, 97, 98, 129; financial status and income, 6, 8, 14-5, 22n, 30, 51, 101, 103-4, 105n, 125-6; gifts from the crown, 7, 8n, 14, 24n, 30-1, 54, 56, 84, 91-2, 104-5, 112-3, 126; annuities, 8n, 22n, 38n, 125n; mercantile interests, 67, 89, 123-5; mining interests, 123-4; estates, 2-4, 14, 30, 56, 84, 92, 99-126; licences to alienate land, 115-6; rental policies, 116-23; religious views, 41-3, 94; will, 42, 99-100, 122; death, 99-100

Russell, John (John's grandfather), 1-2, 3n, 101
Russell, John, clerk of the court of Makesey, 5n
Russell, John, secretary to Princess Mary's Council, 65n
Russell, Sir John of Worcester, 14n
Russell, Stephen, 1-2, 3n
Russell, Thomasine, 2, 3n, 99
Russell, William, 2n
Rutland, Earl of, *see* Manners, Thomas

Sadler, Sir Ralph, 17, 34, 122
St. Albans, monastery of, 106, 108
Samford Courtenay, 71
*Santa Maria de Guadalupe,* 124
Sapcote, Anne, *see* Russell, Anne
Sapcote, Sir Guy, 14, 102
Sapcote, Robert, 38
Sarum, Bishop of, 52
Savoy, Duke of, *see* Charles, Duke of Savoy
Scheyfve, Jehan, Imperial ambassador, 89, 93-4, 124
Scotland: war in 1542, 45-6, 49; during Edward VI's reign, 88
Seymour, Edward, Earl of Hertford and Duke of Somerset: service under Henry VIII, 4, 17, 33, 45, 49, 51; Henry's will, 54-5; lord protector, 55-61, 69-72, 73-4, 82-3, 113, 128; *coup* of 1549, 82-6; during Warwick's ascendancy, 86-8; personality, 52, 54, 82; land disputes with Lord Lisle, 36, 52; relationship with Russell, 44, 52-4, 60, 72, 83-5, 128, 129; estates 113, 126

Seymour, Sir Henry, 83
Seymour, Jane, Queen of England, 23, 31n, 36, 52
Seymour, Thomas, Lord, 17, 48, 56, 59-60, 113
Sheffield, Edmund, Lord, 56
Shitterton (Somerset), 102
Shrewsbury, Earl of, *see* Talbot, Francis and George
Sidney, Sir Henry, 99n
Sidney, Sir Philip, 99n
Slawston (Leicestershire), 107
Smith, Sir Thomas, 82
Somerset, Charles, Earl of Worcester, 7
Somerset, Duke of, *see* Seymour, Edward
Southampton, city of, 75, 98-9
Southampton, Earl of, *see* Fitzwilliam, William and Wriothesley, Thomas
Southwell, Sir Richard, 52, 83, 87
Southwitholme, manor of, 110
Spain: alliance of 1523, 9-10; war with France, 10, 12, 45-8, 89; control of papacy, 18, 20; alliance of 1543, 46; trade disputes, 89, 124; *see also* Charles V; Philip II; Russell, John, attitude toward Spain
Speke, Sir Thomas, 111
Stafford, Edward, Duke of Buckingham, 104
Stamford, 26
Stanley, Henry, Earl of Derby, 99
Stannaries, 30, 39-40, 46, 65, 69, 80-1; *see also* Russell, John, official responsibilities in the west
Stour Provost (Devon), 2, 102
Suffolk, Duke of, *see* Brandon, Charles and Grey, Henry
Surrey, Earl of, *see* Howard, Thomas
Sussex, Earl of, *see* Radcliffe, Henry and Thomas
Swyre (Dorset), 102

Talbot, Francis, fifth Earl of Shrewsbury, 93, 95, 98
Talbot, George, fourth Earl of Shrewsbury, 26-7
Talbot, Sir Gilbert, 5
Tarrant (Dorset), 110
Tavistock, borough of, 36, 40, 80n, 105
Tavistock, estate of, 30, 65, 104-5, 118-23, 125
Tavistock, monastery of, 30, 38, 105, 117-9, 121
Therouanne, 6
Thirlby, Thomas, Bishop of Ely, 98
Thornaugh, manor of, 14
Thorney, monastery of, 113n

Thubianville, captain, 7
Torrigiano, Pietro, 100n
Totnes, 36, 68
Tournai, 6-7, 8, 14, 24, 47
Trenchard, Henry, 4, 38
Trenchard, Sir Thomas, 3-4
Trevanion family, 67
Trevanion, Sir Hugh, 39, 69, 77
Trevanion, Hugh, jr., 39, 122
Tunstall, Cuthbert, Bishop of Durham, 58
Tyler, Sir William, 16

Underhill, Edward, 40-1
Utcott Crawley (Bedfordshire), 113

Venice, 18, 19
Vere, John de, Earl of Oxford, 93
Verona, Bishop of, 36
Veysey, John, Bishop of Exeter : alienation of episcopal lands, 109,
    111-2; relationship with Russell, 38, 111; resignation, 79
Vowell, John, alias John Hooker, 75, 109n

Wallop, Sir John, 16n
Walshe, Robert, 41
Warwick, Earl of, see Dudley, John
Watford (Hertfordshire), 108
Wenton, Robert, 119
Wenton, Thomas, 119
Werrington, manor of, 105, 117-8, 120-3
Werying, Joan, 121
Werying, Richard, 121
Western counties, see Russell, John, official responsibilities in the
    west
Western Uprising of 1549: causes, 60-1, 63, 69-70, 73-4; Russell's
    role, 25, 42, 61, 70-2, 83-4; arguments between Russell and lord
    protector, 72, 84-5; repercussions, 61, 73-81, 112, 122
Westhamptree, manor of, 107
Westley, manor of, 107, 116
Westmorland, Earl of, see Neville, Henry
Weston, Sir Richard, 7
Weston, Sir William, Turcopolier of the Order of St. John, 11
Weymouth, 1-3, 69, 102
Whenacot, John, 121
Whiting, Richard, abbot of Glastonbury, 42

Whitley (Bedfordshire), 113
Wilbraham, Richard, 40
Williams, John, 129
Willoughby, William, Lord, 56
Windsor Castle, 82-3, 86, 92, 95
Wingfield, Sir Richard, 7
Winter, Thomas, 18n, 36
Woburn, manor of, 56-7, 100, 113
Wolsey, Thomas, Cardinal and Archbishop of York: court politics, 7-8; Eltham Ordinances, 13, 16-7; role in foreign affairs, 9-13, 18-21; attitude towards Richard Pace, 13-4; relationship with Russell, 5-9, 13-4, 16-7, 18n, 21-2, 36, 128, 129; fall from power, 21-2, 35
Worcester, Earl of, *see* Somerset, Charles
Wriothesley, Thomas, Earl of Southampton, 46, 55-7, 83, 87, 126
Wyatt, Sir Thomas, the Elder,18-9, 34, 41, 128
Wyatt, Sir Thomas, the Younger, 97, 128
Wyatt's rebellion, 25, 81, 97-9
Wydcombe, manor of, 107
Wyndham, Thomas, 124
Wynterborne-Musterton, manor of, 110
Wyse, Alice, 2, 3n, 38
Wyse, John, 38

York, 26, 45, 70

# Other volumes in this series

1    The Politics of Stability: A Portrait of the Rulers    *Frank F. Foster*
in Elizabethan London

2    The Frankish Church and The Carolingian    *Rosamond McKitterick*
Reforms, 789-895

3    John Burns    *Kenneth D. Brown*

4    Revolution and Counter-Revolution in Scotland,    *David Stevenson*
1644-1651

5    The Queen's Two Bodies: Drama and the    *Marie Axton*
Elizabethan Succession

6    Great Britain and International Security,    *Anne Orde*
1920-1926

7    Legal Records and the Historian    *J. H. Baker (ed.)*

8    Church and State in Independent Mexico:    *Michael P. Costeloe*
A Study of the Patronage Debate 1821-1857

9    An Early Welsh Microcosm: Studies in the    *Wendy Davies*
Llandaff Charters

10    The British in Palestine: The Mandatory    *Bernard Wasserstein*
Government and the Arab-Jewish Conflict

11    Order and Equipoise: The Peerage and the    *Michael McCahill*
House of Lords, 1783-1806

12    Preachers, Peasants and Politics in Southeast    *Norman Etherington*
Africa 1835-1880: African Christian
Communities in Natal, Pondoland and Zululand

13    Linlithgow and India: British Policy and the    *S. A. G. Rizvi*
Political Impasse in India 1936-1943

14    Britain and her Buffer State: The Collapse of the    *David McLean*
Persian Empire, 1890-1914

15    Guns and Government: The Ordnance Office    *Howard Tomlinson*
under the Later Stuarts

16    Denzil Holles 1598-1680: A Study of his Political    *Patricia Crawford*
Career

17    The Parliamentary Agents: A History    *D. L. Rydz*

18    The Shadow of the Bomber: The Fear of Air    *Uri Bialer*
Attack and British Politics 1932-1939

19    La Rochelle and the French Monarchy:    *David Parker*
Conflict and Order in Seventeenth —
Century France

20   The Purchase System in the British Army                    *A. P. C. Bruce*
     1660-1871

21   The Manning of the British Navy during                 *Stephen F. Gradish*
     The Seven Years' War

22   Law-Making and Law-Makers in British History        *Alan Harding (ed.)*

Copies obtainable on order from
Swift Printers (Sales) Ltd., 1-7 Albion Place, Britton Street, London EC1M 5RE